D0369397

THE
WRECK

4-98

	DATE DUE		

363.123
WRE   The wreck of the Titanic
        foretold?

HAYNER PUBLIC LIBRARY DISTRICT
ALTON, ILLINOIS

OVERDUES .10 PER DAY. MAXIMUM FINE
COST OF BOOKS. LOST OR DAMAGED BOOKS
ADDITIONAL $5.00 SERVICE CHARGE.

THE
WRECK
OF THE

TITANIC
foretold?

EDITED BY

MARTIN GARDNER

WITH A NEW PREFACE

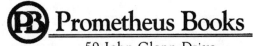 **Prometheus Books**

59 John Glenn Drive
Amherst, New York 14228-2197

HAYNER PUBLIC LIBRARY DISTRICT
ALTON, ILLINOIS

Published 1998 by Prometheus Books

The Wreck of the Titanic Foretold? Copyright © 1998 by Martin Gardner. All rights reserved. No part of this publication may be reproduced, stored in a retrieval system, or transmitted in any form or by any means, electronic, mechanical, photocopying, recording, or otherwise, without prior written permission of the publisher, except in the case of brief quotations embodied in critical articles or reviews. Inquiries should be addressed to Prometheus Books, 59 John Glenn Drive, Amherst, New York 14228-2197, 716-691-0133. FAX: 716–691-0137.

02 01 00 99 98   5 4 3

Library of Congress Cataloging-in-Publication Data

The wreck of the Titanic foretold? / edited by Martin Gardner,
    with a new preface.
        p.   cm.
    Originally published: Buffalo, N.Y. : Prometheus Books, c1986.
    ISBN 1-57392–201-3
    1. Titanic (Steamship) 2. Precognition. 3. Titanic
(Steamship)—Fiction. I. Gardner, Martin, 1914–   .
G530.T6W73   1998
363.12′3—dc21   98–12170
                                                            CIP

Printed in the United States of America on acid-free paper.

36363
WRE

ADC-3816

CONTENTS

Preface to the Paperback Edition   1

Introduction   7

1   The Wreck of the Titan   25

2   From the Old World to the New   89

3   The White Ghost of Disaster   123

4   "A Tryst," and Other Poems   149

v

PREFACE TO THE PAPERBACK EDITION

Since this book first appeared in 1986, public interest in the *Titanic* has been increasing. New books have appeared with such titles as *The Night Lives On,* by Walter Lord; *Her Name: Titanic,* by Charles Pellegrino; *Titanic: An Illustrated History,* by Don Lynch; *The Riddle of the Titanic,* by Robin Gardiner and Dan van der Vat; *Down with the Old Boat,* by Steven Biel; and many, many others.

More than a hundred books have been written about the ill-fated ship. A hundred songs about the disaster were published within a few years after the ship sank. A CBS miniseries featuring George C. Scott as the ship's captain aired on television in 1996. *Titanic,* a musical, opened on Broadway in April 1997. James Cameron's movie *Titanic,* said to be the eighteenth film about the ship, was released in December 1997. Television channels have revived a popular early film on the sinking starring Barbara Stanwyck and Clifton Webb.

As everyone knows, the *Titanic*'s wreckage was found in 1985, and there are even plans to lift it to the surface. Thousands of artifacts have been salvaged, not only gold and silver objects, china, jackets, and jewelry, but also stock certificates, playing cards, and even love letters.

The *New York Times* reported (April 8, 1997) that, contrary to what has been widely believed, the ship did not sink because of an enormous gash in its hull. It sank because of six narrow slits across watertight holds. There is no longer any doubt, again contrary to survivor reports, that the liner broke in half as it plunged bow foremost into the icy sea.

Several minor errors in this book's hardcover edition are here corrected. Other mistakes were impossible to remedy without repagination

1

so let me mention them here. Richard Branham wrote to point out that the photo of the *Titanic* off the coast of France was obviously retouched because it shows an aft funnel (smokestack) belching smoke. This funnel was a dummy, constructed only for show.

Charles P. Chaffe convinced me that "Mayn Clew Garnett," the by-line of a story reprinted in this book, obviously was a pseudonym. A "clew-garnet" is a tackle attached to the clew of a square sail on old sailing ships, used to haul the sail up for furling.

Judy Rehm-Norbo called my attention to a curious coincidence on page 27 that I failed to notice. Morgan Robertson's novella was first published by a firm called Mansfield. The man who reprinted the short novel in 1985 lived in Mansfield, Ohio.

Robertson was a believer in psychic powers. The American poet and spiritualist Ella Wheeler Wilcox, in her second autobiography, *The Worlds and I* (pages 219–21), writes of how struck she was by Robertson's precognition. When the *Titanic* sank, she and her husband were on the *Olympic* headed for England. In England she learned of Robertson's prophetic novel. Curious to know more about the matter, she wrote to the author and received the following reply:

> As to the motif of my story, I merely tried to write a good story with no idea of being a prophet. But, as in other stories of mine, and in the work of other and better writers, coming discoveries and events have been anticipated. I do not doubt that it is because all creative workers get into a hypnoid, telepathic and percipient condition, in which, while apparently awake, they are half asleep, and tap, not only the better informed minds of others but the subliminal realm of unknown facts. Some, as you know, believe that in this realm there is no such thing as Time, and the fact that a long dream can occur in an instant of time gives color to it, and partly explains prophecy.

How, Wilcox wanted to know, could "Mr. Robertson fix on almost the very name which was afterward given to the ill-fated sea monster?" New evidence has recently emerged which makes this coincidence far less astonishing.

Everett Bleiler, in his marvelous reference work *Science Fiction: The Early Years* (Kent State University Press, 1990), reports his discovery of an obscure novel by William Young Winthrop. Nothing is known about Winthrop except that he was born in 1852 and lived in Woodmont, Connecticut. Titled *A 20th Century Cinderella or $20,000*

Reward, Winthrop's novel was published in 1902 by the Abbey Press, a New York vanity house. Bleiler summarizes the plot, calling the book "a very long amateurish novel" and a "silly bore." I mention the novel here only because it refers to a gigantic ocean liner called the *Titanic* that had been built by England's White Star company sometime before 1920, the year in which Winthrop's science-fiction story takes place.

Now the actual *Titanic* was also a White Star liner, although not built until a decade after Winthrop's novel was published! This could be another coincidence (believers in precognition will no doubt consider it another paranormal prophecy even though the fictional *Titanic* does not sink), but does it not suggest the following? It seems to me entirely possible that the White Star company, as early as 1898, when Robertson wrote his novel, had announced plans to construct the world's largest ocean liner and to call it the *Titanic.*

Even more relevant is a quotation from *Titanic: Destination Disaster* (1987), by John P. Eaton and Charles Hass, which was sent to me by Mrs. Brenda Bright. The authors reproduce in its entirety the following news item from the September 17, 1892, issue of the *New York Times.* This was six years before Robertson's novel was published:

> London, Sept. 16—The White Star Company has commissioned the great Belfast shipbuilders Harland and Wolff to build an Atlantic steamer that will beat the record in size and speed.
>
> She has already been named *Gigantic,* and will be 700 feet long, 65 feet 7½ inches beam and 45,000 horsepower. It is calculated that she will steam 22 knots an hour, with a maximum speed of 27 knots. She will have three screws, two fitted like *Majestic*'s, and the third in the centre. She is to be ready for sea in March, 1894.

The figures given for the planned liner are very close to those Robertson used for his imaginary *Titan.* The *Gigantic* was to be 700 feet long, with 45,000 horsepower, a speed of 22 to 27 knots, and three propellers. The Titan was 800 feet long, 40,000 horsepower (changed to 75,000 in the book's second printing), a speed of 25 knots when it struck the iceberg, and with three propellers.

The *Gigantic* was never built. At the time Robertson wrote his novel the White Star had built the *Oceanic* (1871), the *Britannic* (1874), the *Teutonic* (1889), and the *Majestic* (1889). The company always added "ic" to the names of its liners. After Robertson's novel was published it would build a second *Oceanic,* a *Celtic, Cedric, Baltic, Adriatic, Olympic,* and *Titanic.*

It seems clear now what happened. Knowing of plans for the *Gigantic,* Robertson modeled his ship on this proposed mammoth liner. After the use of such names as *Oceanic, Teutonic, Majestic,* and *Gigantic,* what appropriate name is left for a giant liner except *Titanic?* Not wishing to identify his doomed *Titan* with the White Star line, Robertson dropped "ic" from the name. The White Star's later choice of *Titanic* for its 1910 ship was almost inevitable. The company was surely aware of Robertson's *Titan,* but perhaps did not mind adopting a similar name because it was firmly persuaded that its *Titanic* was absolutely unsinkable.

A raft of old poems about the *Titanic* has come to light, enough to make a book anthology. One of the worst was four stanzas of doggerel by Chicago writer Ben Hecht, which Walter Lord includes in *The Night Lives On,* a sequel to his memorable *A Night to Remember.* I will inflict on the reader only the first stanza:

> The Captain stood where a captain should
> For the law of the sea is grim.
>   The owner romped ere his ship was swamped
> And no law bothered him.

A much better poem, though with a regrettable racist line in the second stanza, was written by, of all people, Sir Arthur Conan Doyle. Doyle and George Bernard Shaw clashed over how one should react to the *Titanic* disaster. Their argumentative letters to a British newspaper were reprinted in *ACD,* the journal of the Arthur Conan Doyle Society (vol. 5, 1994, pages 127–49), with commentary and annotations by Doug Elliot. (I am grateful to Dana Richards for a copy.) Learning that the band played ragtime to keep up the passenger's spirits, Doyle was moved to write the following poem which he titled "Ragtime!"

> Ragtime! Ragtime! Keep it going still!
> Let them hear the ragtime! Play it with a will!
> Women in the lifeboats, men upon the wreck,
> Take heart to hear the ragtime lilting down the deck.

> Ragtime! Ragtime! Yet another tune!
> Now the 'Darkey Dandy,' now 'The Yellow Coon!'
> Brace against the bulwarks if the stand's askew,
> Find your footing as you can, but keep the music true!

There's glowing hell beneath us where the shattered boilers roar,
The ship is listing and awash, the boats will hold no more!
There's nothing more that you can do, and nothing you can mend,
Only keep the ragtime playing to the end.

Don't forget the time, boys! Eyes upon the score!
Never heed the wavelets sobbing down the floor!
Play it as you played it when with eager feet
A hundred pairs of dancers were stamping to the beat.

Stamping to the ragtime down the lamp-lit deck,
With shine of glossy linen and with gleam of snowy neck,
They've other thoughts to think to-night, and other things to do,
But the tinkle of the ragtime may help to see them through.

Shut off, shut off the ragtime! The lights are falling low!
The deck is buckling under us! She's sinking by the bow!
One hymn of hope from dying hands on dying ears to fall—
Gently the music fades away—and so, God rest us all!

Lord devotes an entire chapter, "The Sound of Music," to the *Titanic*'s band. "The last moments of the Titanic," he writes, "are full of mysteries—none more intriguing than those surrounding the ship's band. We know they played, but little else. Where they played, how long they played, and what they played remain matters for speculation." As I said in my first introduction, not one of the eight musicians survived.

The White Star Company, I earlier noted, ended the names of its liners with "ic." Its rival Cunard Company ended its ships' names with "ia." If it had built the *Titanic*, Richard Branham speculated in a letter, the ship might have been called *Titania*. Branham also pointed out numerous coincidences involving Robertson's *Titan* and the *Lusitania*. The *Titan* sank in April of an unspecified year. The *Lusitania* was torpedoed and sunk in May 1915. The *Titan*'s captain was named Bryce. The chief engineer of the *Lusitania* was Archie Bryce. The *Lusitania*'s dimensions were actually closer to those of the *Titan* than to the *Titanic*. Branham, tongue in cheek, makes out as good a case for Robertson precognizing the *Lusitania* disaster as for anticipating the *Titanic*'s sinking.

One of the most moving accounts of the *Titanic* tragedy was written by Elbert Hubbard. You'll find excerpts in *Elbert Hubbard of East Aurora*, a 1926 biography by Felix Shay (pages 513–20). Hubbard concluded his essay by writing, "One thing sure, there are just two respectable ways to die. One is of old age, and the other is by accident.

All disease is indecent. Suicide is atrocious. But to pass out, as did Mr. and Mrs. Isador Straus, is glorious. Few have such a privilege. Happy lovers, both. In life they were never separated, and in death they are not divided."

On May 7, 1915, Elbert Hubbard and his wife Alice perished in the sinking of the *Lusitania.*

INTRODUCTION

There are few persons, even among the calmest thinkers, who have not occasionally been startled into a vague yet thrilling half-credence in the supernatural, by *coincidences* of so seemingly marvellous a character that, as *mere* coincidences, the intellect has been unable to receive them. Such sentiments—for the half-credences of which I speak have never the full force of *thought*—such sentiments are seldom thoroughly stifled unless by reference to the doctrine of chance, or, as it is technically termed, the Calculus of Probabilities. Now this Calculus is, in its essence, purely mathematical; and thus we have the anomaly of the most rigidly exact in science applied to the shadow and spirituality of the most intangible in speculation.

Edgar Allan Poe, "The Mystery of Marie Roget"

Poe's lines express an emotion that almost all persons experience at some time in their lives. Over and over again, when the topic of the paranormal comes up in conversation, someone is compelled to recount, often in exasperating detail, an instance from the past when he or she was shaken by a coincidence so extraordinary that it seems impossible to believe it was chance. "How do you explain *that?*" will be flung at any skeptical listener. No amount of talk about probability and statistics is likely to have any effect on the person's convictions. The great coincidence has left an indelible impression. I suspect it would be hard to find a parapsychologist whose interest in the field was not strongly stimulated by one or more such personal experiences.

Before discussing the question central to this strange anthology—was the *Titanic* disaster foreseen by extrasensory perception?—let us take a look at coincidences in general. The single most important thing to understand is that in most cases of startling coincidences it is impossible to make even a rough estimate of their probability. They are what mathematicians call problems that are not "well formed."

Consider, for example, the most common type of precognition—the precognitive dream. There simply is no way to evaluate the degree to which such a dream runs counter to ordinary statistical laws.

Most dreams contain a wealth of vaguely defined, unrelated events. It is impossible to know how many events in a precognitive dream were quickly forgotten because they had no relation to any waking events in the near future. Assume a woman dreams that her Aunt Mary dies in a fire. In the same dream Aunt Mary's husband escapes the fire by jumping out a window and breaks a leg. A few days later one of the following events takes place: Aunt Mary dies of an illness, her husband breaks his arm in an auto accident, or a house in the neighborhood catches on fire. If Aunt Mary dies, the dreamer will be able to tell friends that only a few days ago she dreamed that her aunt died. If the husband breaks an arm, the dreamer may recall that in her dream he broke one of his bones, she isn't sure which, but she *thinks* it was his arm. And of course if a house nearby catches fire she will recall *that* aspect of the dream. Other events in the same dream, of which there could be scores, will be totally unremembered. Even if the dream stressed only the three events mentioned, the mere presence of all three raises the probability of a meaningful correlation.

The probability of at least one meaningful correlation rises even more steeply when we consider the time-lag between a precognitive dream and the event. Many such dreams occur several days, sometimes even weeks, before the dramatic event. This means we have to consider all the events that occurred in all of the person's dreams over what may be a substantial number of days. Because there is no way to retrieve the hundreds of events that may have occurred in dreams during the period preceding the event, the task of estimating the probability of one correlation is hopeless.

There is still more to consider. Every night, all over the world, billions of people are dreaming. Is it not obvious that the probability of remarkable correlations of dream events and future events occurring in *some* of these billions of dreams is extremely high? Of course, whenever an extraordinary correlation does turn up, there is certain to be an intense, unshakable feeling of improbability in the mind of the dreamer.

With respect to dreams about major disasters that make the head-lines, we have no inkling of the millions and millions of times that people dream of such a disaster and nothing happens. You can be sure that every time a great liner sets sail or a huge plane takes off with many passengers it is not unlikely that at least one passenger, or a relative of a passenger, will dream of a sinking ship or an airplane crash. Once the ship or plane has arrived safely, who would mention such a dream or even recall it? But if a disaster does occur, such a dream is at once remembered and passed down in families to children and grandchildren. Earthquakes and floods are less likely to figure in disaster dreams for the obvious reason that no one can fix a time frame for such events. One is much more likely to have an unconscious fear that a loved one will die on a specified air flight than a fear that that person will die in an earthquake. Nevertheless, it would be interesting to know, as of course we cannot, how often there are dreams of earthquakes in California. For all we know there could be thousands every month. Eventually an earthquake is sure to occur. When it does, anyone who dreamed of an earthquake in the near past will remember it and there will be an irresistible impulse to regard the dream as precognitive.

Finally, it is worth remembering that after any major disaster there is a curious type of person, anxious to gain recognition in a community, who will lie about a precognitive dream. If the person is a professional psychic or has a reputation among friends of being psychic, the temptation to fabricate such a dream, or to exaggerate a dream, will be strong. Even among people who are completely honest there will be a tendency to exaggerate without realizing it. After telling about a precognitive dream for the umpteenth time, one no longer recalls the dream's actual details, especially if it occurred many years ago. Dreams are hard enough to remember accurately ten minutes after waking! One is soon recalling not the dream itself but pictures that formed in the mind during previous tellings. The only way a precognitive disaster dream can have evidential value is when its details are written down before a disaster and dated in a way that can be verified, such as being described in a letter or published before the event or stated on a radio or television talk-show.

It is extraordinarily difficult for most people to grasp the fact that *some* improbable events are extremely probable, and in some cases absolutely certain. If you buy a ticket for the Irish sweepstakes, the probability *you* will win is extremely low. But the probability *someone* will win is certain. If you lose, you have no difficulty understanding why. But, if you win, the impulse to attribute this good fortune to something paranormal is hard to resist. Perhaps God answered a prayer. Perhaps the ticket's number had some special meaning—its digits coincided with a phone number, a birthdate, a house number, a zip code, part of your social security number, a number you dreamed about, or a dozen other possibilities. If your number differs in only one digit from the winning number, you may feel that the Fates are going out of their way to tease you. The impression will be that you came extremely close to winning, whereas, in fact, every losing number was just as "close" to winning as yours.

Whenever there are a multitude of possible ways in which a coincidence can occur, the occasional appearance of a strong coincidence is not surprising. This frequently happens in scientific investigations. One of the most difficult of all problems involving scientific method is finding good ways to evaluate unusual patterns of data to determine if they are based on a law of nature or are no more than the normally expected anomalies of random coincidence.

Sometimes what is believed to be a coincidence turns out not to be. An excellent example of this is the way the eastern coasts of the Americas seem to fit the western coasts of Europe and Africa. Geologists thought this a coincidence until evidence became overwhelming that a single continent had split and its two sides had drifted apart. When the atomic weights of elements were found to be exact multiples of the atomic weight of hydrogen, some chemists thought this a coincidence. It turned out not to be. It seemed a remarkable coincidence that the gravitational mass of a falling object exactly equals its inertial mass until the equivalence was explained by Einstein's general theory of relativity.

Cases like these, and there are endless others, are balanced by cases in which a startling coincidence is really nothing but coincidental. My favorite example is the fact that the sun's disk is almost exactly the same size as the moon's. Moreover, the moon goes around the earth in about 30 days, and the sun rotates on its axis in about the same period. The diameter of the earth's orbit is about 186,000,000 miles, and light travels at close to 186,000 miles per second. Taken in isolation, anomalies like these seem remarkable. Taken in the context of the billions of ways that scientific data can have accidental correlations, they are unremarkable.

A failure to appreciate the frequency of unusual patterns, when the number of possible patterns is large, has an obvious bearing on the claims of parapsychology. It has been pointed out many times that enormous numbers of ESP tests go unreported because the results are negative. In the light of the total number of such tests made around the world, one would expect a certain proportion, by laws of chance alone, to show unusual correlations. If large numbers of tests go unreported, the illusion that ESP is behind the published anomalies is enormously strengthened.

Professional soothsayers, especially the out-and-out charlatans, are well aware of the importance of making many predictions. They know their misses will be quickly forgotten and their hits widely publicized. Studies of the thousands of predictions that have been made by Jeane Dixon show such a poor record of hits that I'm surprised no one has suggested that "negative psi" may be the cause. But, when only her successes are listed, the illusion that she can foresee the future is strong. Psychics who claim to solve crimes use a similar technique. They will talk at police headquarters for hours, rattling off a hundred "impressions" about the crime. If among them there are lucky hits, naive police officers and gullible newspaper reporters will be enormously impressed.

Suppose you get a phone call from a stranger who says he knows the winning horse in a forthcoming race. It turns out that the horse wins. Later you get a second call from the same man, giving the winner in another race. He is right again. The third time he calls, he offers to sell you the name of the next winner. Should you buy it? Not if you know what actually has been going on. For the first race, in which seven horses ran, the man called seventy people, taking their names at random from a phone book. The first ten were given the name of horse *A;* the second ten, the name of horse *B;* and so on. Of course ten people will have been told the winner. Ten horses were in the second race. The man then called the ten who got the correct name for the first race. He gives each the name of a different horse. Of course one person got the winning name. Now he calls this person a third time with an offer to sell. Not knowing the background data, you would be inclined to estimate the probability of chance explaining the first two calls as a low 1/70.

Science-fiction writers are often given more credit than they deserve for remarkable predictions. H. G. Wells, for instance, in *The World Set Free,* opens with a description of how the atom was split. The chapter is an astonishing prophecy of what actually happened. In addition, Wells has a world war occurring in the mid-forties in which "atom bombs" are dropped. Considering that novel alone, one might suppose Wells was gifted with paranormal foresight. But Wells made thousands of other predictions in his books, most of which were misses. He saw no future for submarines in warfare, for example, and even in *The World Set Free* he has atom bombs dropped by hand through a hole in the bottom of a plane. Considering the millions of stories about the future that have been written, it is perhaps surprising there are not more lucky hits. Lots of science-fiction writers made the safe prediction that astronauts would one day walk on the moon. So far as I know, only a few writers guessed that the first moon-walk would be watched on earth by television.

With respect to extraordinary coincidences in daily life, there is no doubt that many more occur than are recognized. Unless a coincidence is obvious, we miss it simply by not looking for it. I recall an occasion when my wife and I were driving through a strange town. We mentioned somebody's name a block or two before pulling up to a stop light. I noticed that the street had the same name as the person we were discussing. How many people bother to notice the name of every side street they pass in a car? If they did, dozens of unlikely word correlations would be turning up.

Gilbert Chesterton, in a delightful essay on coincidences (in *Alarms and Discursions*) said it this way:

> Life is full of a ceaseless shower of small coincidences; too small to be worth mentioning except for a special purpose, often too trifling even to be noticed, any more than we notice one snowflake falling on another. It is this that lends a frightful plausibility to all false doctrines and evil fads. There are always such props of accidental arguments upon anything. If I said suddenly that historical truth is generally told by red-haired men, I have no doubt that ten minutes' reflection (in which I decline to indulge) would provide me with a handsome list of instances in support of it. I remember a riotous argument about Bacon and Shakespeare in which I offered quite at random to show that Lord Rosebery had written the words of Mr. W. B. Yeats. No sooner had I said the words than a torrent of

coincidences rushed upon my mind. I pointed out, for instance, that Mr. Yeats's chief work was "The Secret Rose." This may easily be paraphrased as "The Quiet or Modest Rose"; and so, of course, as the Primrose. A second after I saw the same suggestion in the combination of "rose" and "bury." If I had pursued the matter, who knows but I might have been a raving maniac by this time.

Because of my interest in strange and amusing coincidences (you'll find hundreds in *The Magic Numbers of Dr. Matrix*), I tend to notice them in my own life more than most people do. I can't recall ever having had a hotel or motel room number I could not easily memorize because of some coincidence: it was a prime, or the power of a number, or a sequence of some sort (such as 3, 6, 9), or the first decimal digits of pi or *e* or some other familiar irrational number. I find a note in my files that on November 21, 1979, I opened a water bill that said I owed $21.21. Clearly the odds against this triplet of 21s is high, but there are so many ways meaningless patterns can show up in random numbers that if you start looking for them you'll find them all over the place.

On March 15, 1977, when Jimmy Carter was president, the *New York Times* printed the following story:

> **James Earl Carter** is his name. He wears blue jeans, he's a former Georgia peanut farmer, he attends a Baptist church, and he has a daughter named Amy who goes to a public school. But he does not live in the White House. This Mr. Carter is an electrician whose home now is in the New Orleans suburb of Kenner, La. Yes, "everybody jokes about it, and all I can tell them is that as far as I know I'm not related to *him*," said Mr. Carter.

In one of my Dr. Matrix columns in *Scientific American* I spoofed the notion that a model of the Great Pyramid contained psychic forces. I had my numerologist manufacturing pyramids at a spot near Pyramid Lake in Arizona, and I mentioned that it might do President Nixon some good to go there and sit on one of the lake's pyramidal rock structures. Jeffrey Mishlove, who believes in paranormal synchronicity and almost everything else on the psi scene, mentions this column in his *Roots of Consciousness,* one of the wildest books on the paranormal ever published. Mishlove thinks he has hoisted me on my own petard. "On the very day that Gardner's article reached the public," he writes, "newspapers throughout the country carried pictures of President Nixon visiting the Great Pyramid in Egypt—a suddenly arranged visit presumably unknown to Gardner when he wrote his story! Such a synchronicity seems to embody the message that even the skeptical joker is part of the 'cosmic puzzle.'" Mishlove seems to think I should be embarrassed by this. My own sarcasm, he writes, "is the very model of psychic synchronicity."

Well, we poor skeptics seldom win. I'm surprised Mishlove has never credited me with psychic power since I had Dr. Matrix successfully predict the millionth decimal of pi long before it had been determined by a computer program.

Magicians and fake psychics are skilled in taking advantage of coincidences. There are dozens of ways to duplicate a drawing by trickery, but a psychic occasionally will take a chance and not cheat at all. He will draw a picture of some object—picking something he knows from experience people often select (such as a house, a ship, a cat, and so on). He will put the drawing face down on a table, then ask a person to draw anything he or she wishes. The psychic's drawing may be correct only about once in twenty times; but, when it is, the person will be convinced for life that the psychic had paranormal powers. Without knowing the background of misses, there is no way to estimate the probability that such a matching is not pure chance.

When I was a sailor in World War II, I sometimes entertained shipmates with card tricks. I often began by removing a card (picking a card often named, such as an ace or a face card) and handing it to someone with the request that he not look at its face until he has called out the name of any card that pops into his mind. If the card was not correctly named I would take it back, glance at it myself (not letting anyone else see the face), exclaim "You're absolutely right!" and then put it back in the deck. This always got a laugh and would be taken as a joke. Of course I was bound to hit more often than 1 in 52 tries. I'll never forget one occasion when a sailor said, "Jack of Hearts," and I asked him to turn the card over slowly. It was the Jack of Hearts. His face turned beet red. No doubt he has since told his grandchildren about the stupendous miracle that a strange sailor showed him more than 40 years ago.

In 1977 a Japanese mathematician wrote to me about an astonishing coincidence that had occurred on an educational television program. A distinguished mathematician at Keio University was explaining elementary probability to junior high school students. To illustrate a point he had his assistant toss in the air eight poker chips, each one red on one side and white on the other. All eight fell with the same color up! You can imagine how shaken the professor must have been. The probability of such an event is $\frac{1}{2}^7$ or a bit under .008. If a psychic had been present, he would have taken credit for influencing the chips by psychokinesis, but of course unlikely events like this are certain to happen sometime.

Random events often display what mathematicians call clustering, clumping, or bunching. It explains many examples of synchronicity that Arthur Koestler stresses in his book *Coincidence*. If you fling a thousand beans on a table they will distribute themselves in clumps, and this kind of clumping is often mistaken, both in science and in daily life, as a nonchance pattern. You can demonstrate the effect by shuffling a deck of cards, then spreading the deck to see how the colors are distributed. You'll be surprised at how often there will be a large bunch of adjacent cards, all the same color. An even more dramatic demonstration is to obtain a large supply of tiny spheres of two colors. Mix equal amounts of the two colors together and pour the mixture into a bottle with transparent sides. The pattern you see will exhibit such marked clumping that even physicists may suspect static attraction between spheres of the same color.

Normal clumping can be extremely misleading in statistical research. A town, for example, suddenly shows a high incidence of cancer. Is there something at work in the local area to cause this, or is it just random clustering? Astronomers find a large patch of space where there are no stars, or a long chain of galaxies. Are natural laws at work, or is it just clumping? It is sometimes difficult to tell. At the time I write (fall 1985), there have been an unusual number of airline disasters. All sorts of speculations are going around, but it is probably just normal clumping.

A parapsychologist reports an unusual number of hits (or misses) in a run of 100 trials. ESP or clumping? It is impossible to tell without knowing how many tests were made, not only by that parapsychologist but also by others around the world. If a thousand scientists, in different parts of the world, toss a hundred pennies in the air, some of the outcomes will show an astonishing number of heads. If only these tests are reported, and we have no knowledge of the others, it will be impossible to make an accurate evaluation of the reported tests. Of course all this applies to statistical research in other areas of science as well. The pitfalls are manifold and subtle. Unless an experiment can be successfully replicated many times, the results may be nothing more than a statistical anomaly. Extraordinary claims for new laws of science demand extraordinary evidence.

With this as background, let us now turn to premonitions of great disasters. Whenever there is a major earthquake, or flood, or fire, or volcanic eruption, or an assassination of a public figure, there are always psychics who will claim to have predicted it, and people who will say they dreamed about it before it happened or had a strong premonition of the event. How much reliance can be placed on such claims?

First we must consider the possibility of fraud. A certain number of psychics will go to any lengths to fake a prediction. When these are discounted, there remain cases where successful predictions actually were recorded. Again, the evaluation of probability is difficult. The problem is not well formed because we don't know how many predictions were recorded in some manner and failed. One by-product of the enormous current wave of interest in the occult is the still-growing number of professional psychics on the scene. They make predictions constantly—on the radio, in letters, on television, in newspapers. It is hardly surprising that, out of the thousands of recorded predictions made every year, some turn out to be remarkable hits. I doubt if a year has gone by in the past few decades that a psychic, somewhere, has not predicted a major California earthquake. When the big quake finally comes, as it must, any psychic who predicted it will get credit, and all his or her misses will be forgotten.

Let us turn to the sinking of the *Titanic*. Although only 1,522 or so people lost their lives, as compared with the tens of thousands in the last great Chinese earthquake, the story of the ship's disaster had many elements that made it unusually newsworthy. The *Titanic* was supposed to be unsinkable. It was a palatial liner on which some of the world's wealthiest people had booked passage for the ship's maiden voyage. A combination of careless events produced the disaster. The captain ignored warnings of icebergs. The ship's speed was increased to meet its scheduled arrival. The ship was inadequately supplied with lifeboats. The crew was untrained for emergencies. Lookouts were not given binoculars. A radio operator in a nearby ship was asleep and failed to receive the SOS. Another nearby ship did not respond soon enough when they learned of the sinking. No person or group could be singled out for blame. More than any other disaster of the time, the *Titanic*'s sinking raised in stark form the old unanswerable question for any theist—why would God allow such a senseless loss of life to happen?

The person who has been the most influential in spreading the view that there were widespread psychic premonitions of the *Titanic* disaster is Dr. Ian Stevenson, professor of psychiatry at the University of Virginia School of Medicine, in Charlottesville. Stevenson's answer to the problem of evil is reincarnation. He is best known in occult circles for his many books and articles about efforts to prove, over several decades, that some people have genuine memories of past lives. From his point of view, the law of Karma is a law of the universe. Evils that occur are part of the process by which souls evolve upward through a succession of perhaps endless lives. This, however, is not the place to discuss reincarnation. We will consider only Stevenson's two published papers on the *Titanic*.

His first paper, "A Review and Analysis of Paranormal Experiences Connected with the Sinking of the *Titanic*," appeared in the *Journal of the American Society for Psychical Research* (vol. 54, October 1960). He opens by recalling an earlier paper in the same journal (July 1956) titled "Precognition: An Analysis, II," by W. E. Cox. (Cox is best known today for his tireless efforts to prove that Uri Geller's psychic powers are genuine.) In his 1956 paper, Cox reported a survey of 28 serious railway accidents in the United States. The raw data, Cox claimed, show that on the days of the accidents significantly fewer people rode the doomed trains. As Cox reasoned, and as Stevenson reemphasizes, unconscious precognition seemed to be at work causing travelers to defer their trip without being aware of their extrasensory perception of the coming accident.

"A considerable number of apparently extrasensory experiences occurred in connection with the dramatic sinking of the White Star Liner *Titanic* in April, 1912," Stevenson continues. "Some of these were apparently precognitive; others, instances of apparent extrasensory perception contemporaneous with the tragedy." He then proceeds to give a brief history of the disaster, followed by summaries of the "most substantial paranormal experiences connected with the disaster."

A footnote makes clear that he is not convinced that "all the experiences I shall review include paranormal cognition." He thinks some show it, while others do not.

Stevenson's first, and by far his best, example of precognition is the short novel by Morgan Robertson, *Futility,* a small book published in 1898, fourteen years before the *Titanic* sank. Stevenson is impressed by ten ways in which the sinking of Robertson's imaginary ship, the *Titan,* parallels the sinking of the *Titanic.* I shall say no more about the parallels here because I shall be discussing them at length in my introduction to *The Wreck of the Titan,* reprinted in full in this anthology. Stevenson's Experiences 2 through 8 are of the anecdotal sort. Let us look briefly at each.

Experience 2. A Mr. Middleton cancels his passage on the *Titanic* after a cable from the United States advises him to do so for business reasons. According to his family and friends, Middleton had two dreams before the disaster in which he saw the liner sink. Because fears of ships hitting icebergs in the North Atlantic were prevalent at the time, dreams of this sort must have been extremely common. In his first dream, Middleton saw the *Titanic* floating keel upward. As Stevenson notes, the liner sank bow upward. He sees discrepancies like this as characteristic of most precognitive dreams. The event gets distorted in the dream.

Experience 3. A New York woman awakens her husband on the night of the *Titanic*'s sinking to tell him she dreamed her mother was in a crowded lifeboat. The mother had not told her daughter she had booked passage on the *Titanic.* The mother survived the disaster. This seems impressive until we learn that the account comes from a book called *The Mystery of Dreams* (1949), in which the author, W. O. Stevens, does not even tell us the names of the mother and daughter! Stevenson is reduced to referring to the daughter as "Mr. Stevens' friend."

Experience 4 is not much better. Mrs. Marshall watches the *Titanic* sail by her home on the Isle of Wight. She clutches her daughter's hand and says, "That ship is going to sink before she reaches America." This childhood memory of her mother's remark is recalled by her daughter in her book *Far Memory* (1956).

Experience 5 is Mrs. Potter's dream. There is no vision of water, merely "something like an elevated railroad" with people hanging from it in nightclothes. When Mrs. Potter later saw an artist's rendering of the *Titanic* going down, she said, "That is just what I saw." This is from her book *Beyond the Senses* (1939).

Experience 6. The minister of a Methodist church feels compelled to have his congregation sing the hymn "Hear, Father, while we pray to Thee, for those in peril on the sea." According to *You Do Take It With You,* a book by R. de W. Miller (1955), while the congregation sang this hymn, passengers in the Second Class dining room of the Titanic were singing the same hymn two hours before the ship struck the iceberg.

Experience 7. Mr. Hays, a passenger on the *Titanic,* is reported to have said before the accident that the time had come for a great sea disaster. (This is like saying today that the time has come for an earthquake in California.) Unfortunately, after the iceberg was hit, Mr. Hays's precognitive powers deserted him, because he said, "You cannot sink this boat." A little later he added, "This ship is good for eight hours." The ship sank in less than two hours. Why Stevenson bothered to list this beats me.

Experience 8. A psychic named Turvey is said to have predicted "a great liner will be lost." He sent his prediction in a letter to a lady who reported it in the spiritualist journal *Light* (June 29, 1912).

Experiences 9 through 12 all involve the famous British journalist and spiritualist W. T. Stead. I will comment on them later in an introduction to two excerpts from Stead's novel.

These are Stevenson's twelve best cases, and I think anyone who considers them carefully will agree that only the first, Robertson's novel, can be viewed as extraordinary. Stevenson adds a few miscellaneous experiences that are even weaker. A Miss Evans, who drowned in the disaster, reportedly tells someone that "a fortune-teller had once told her to 'beware of the water.' " A crewman deserts the *Titanic* when it stops at Queenstown. "As he did not leave a record of his motives," Stevenson remarks, "we can only surmise that these might have included a foreknowledge, perhaps unconscious, of the forthcoming disaster." A military aide to President Taft, Major Butt, writes a letter on February 12 to tell his sister not to forget where he stored his papers in case the "old ship goes down." Unfortunately, he wrote this before going to Europe on the S.S. *Berlin,* but he returned on the *Titanic* and was among those who perished. The anecdote comes from

The Intimate Letters of Archie Butt, in two volumes (1930).

Stevenson is aware of how weak most of his twelve cases are. They lack "much that we would wish in the way of further details," especially "contemporary affidavits from witnesses" that recorded premonitions prior to news of the ship's sinking. In fact, Stevenson goes at some length to argue that even the novels by Robertson and Stead can easily be considered cases of what he calls "reasonable inference" rather than precognition. Nevertheless, Stevenson presents his cases as though they add up to significant evidence for ESP. His final conclusion is admirably cautious: "We shall never know, but possibly some of these persons behaved sensibly (as proven by the subsequent sinking) in response to an unconscious precognition while attributing their behavior to an irrational belief."

In spite of these cautions, Stevenson was sufficiently interested in the possibility of psychic perception of the *Titanic* disaster to write a second paper: "Seven More Paranormal Experiences Associated with the Sinking of the *Titanic"* (same journal, vol. 59, July 1965).

Experience 13. In 1919 the *Journal of the American Society for Psychical Research* printed a letter received several weeks after the *Titanic* went down. The writer, not named, claims he had a dream on the night of April 14 in which his deceased father appeared to tell him that a ship had hit an iceberg with much loss of life. "Corroborations are not given," said the author of the article in which the letter was printed, "but a trusted member of the Society knows Mr. M. well and considers him reliable."

Experience 14. Mrs. Henry Sidgwick, an ardent spiritualist (as was her husband, a famous British philosopher), tells in a 1923 article about a letter she received from someone who asked that pseudonyms be substituted for all actual names. The letter (dated July 4, 1912) tells of a friend of the writer who lost a brother on the *Titanic.* It seems that on April 19, a few days after the disaster, the sister of the friend saw in a dream the wife and daughter of the doomed man. They were crying. At the time, it is claimed, the sister who had the dream did not know her brother was on the *Titanic.* Since we don't know the names of anyone involved, and Mrs. Sidgwick is reporting a letter from a woman who in turn is reporting what a friend told her about a dream of the friend's sister, the anecdote seems hardly worth mentioning.

Experience 15. Stevenson prints a letter from an actor in White

Cloud, Michigan. The actor recalls a dream by his associate Mr. Black, in which Black said he saw a large ship sinking and hundreds of people drowning. Later that day a telegraph agent tells them about the hundreds who died in the *Titanic* disaster. Stevenson discloses that reports on April 15 were optimistic, and that the telegraph agent could not have known of the drowning of "hundreds." But, Stevenson adds, the agent "may have had some extrasensory perception of the disaster, for which the telegraphic news acted as a kind of nucleus and stimulus for conscious expression." Note how Stevenson, never questioning the reliability of the actor's memory, stretches the anecdote to the limit to account for a serious discrepancy in the story.

Experience 16. When Stevenson was in Brazil in 1962 he met a man who told him about his mother's paranormal perception of the *Titanic*'s sinking. He had heard the story from his father. According to the father, on the night of the disaster his wife had a dream in which she said she saw a big ship called the *Titanic* sink after hitting an iceberg. How did Stevenson corroborate this? Why, he later heard from the informant's sister, who was four years old at the time of the disaster, that the story was accurate!

Experience 17. An English woman writes to Stevenson to tell him about a dream she had when she was fourteen. In the dream she saw a large ship sinking in a waterless park near her home. A few days later came the news that her uncle, an engineer on the *Titanic,* had drowned. Stevenson points out some discrepancies. The woman said they learned of the uncle's death when they saw his picture in the *Daily Mirror* on the morning of April 15. The picture actually appeared on May 4 in an illustrated magazine called *Sphere.* No morning newspaper of April 15 carried the story because the news had not yet reached England.

Experience 18. Stevenson gets a letter from a woman who recalls a premonition she had when she was eleven. Her mother, Mrs. Roberts, was about to sail on the *Titanic* as a stewardess. The daughter begged her mother not to go because she had a strong feeling of disaster. Her mother went anyway, and was a survivor. The woman also told Stevenson that on a later occasion she tried to stop her mother from sailing on a hospital ship. Again the mother did not heed the warning, the ship sank, and she escaped a second time. Stevenson adds that a Mrs. Roberts was on the *Titanic*'s crew list, but he reports no effort to verify her later escape from the sinking of a hospital ship.

Experience 19. A newspaper obit of one Colin Macdonald, who died in 1963, said he had refused to join the *Titanic's* engineering crew because of a premonition of disaster. Stevenson looked up the man's daughter. Yes, she told him, her father had a hunch not to go on the ship.

Weak as these additional cases are, Stevenson seems impressed by the fact that more such cases turn up about the *Titanic* than about disasters involving greater loss of life. Why? He thinks that the "sudden, unexpected anticipation of death generated a greater than usual amount of emotion. . . . We have evidence from many other studies of spontaneous cases and from laboratory experiments that strength of emotion is an important feature in . . . extrasensory perception." Stevenson also believes that his nineteen cases show that "sleep for many people provides better conditions for extrasensory perception than does the waking state." Discrepancies are explained by the fact that "in physical perceptions the veridical details become distorted or blended with other details associated in the mind of the percipient."

In spite of skeptical remarks here and there, there is little question that Stevenson thinks his nineteen cases provide impressive evidence for ESP. Here is how he summarizes his opinion in an article on premonitions of disasters in the *Journal of the American Society for Psychical Research* for April 1970. "I was able to assemble a considerable number of corroborated reports suggesting that these nineteen percipients had had extrasensory awareness of the sinking of the *Titanic*. Ten of the cases were precognitive."

I mentioned earlier that Stevenson wondered why there were so many more cases on record of ESP involving the *Titanic* than in connection with worse disasters, including the sinking of the *Lusitania* in 1915. His 1970 paper repeats his earlier expressed opinion that, unlike the *Lusitania* and loss of life in military battles, the *Titanic* sinking was "totally unexpected. . . . I suggest that the very unexpectedness of the sinking of the *Titanic* may have generated an emotional shock not present in disasters that are less surprising. . . ."

In the same paper Stevenson reports on a study by the English psychiatrist J. C. Barker (*Journal of the Society for Psychical Research,* December 1967) of no less than 35 precognitive accounts "worthy of confidence" about a disaster in Aberfan, Wales, in 1966, when a slag heap slid down a mountainside, killing 144 persons.

Stevenson recognizes that anecdotal evidence of this sort is less reliable than laboratory experiments. "Perhaps the best evidence for precognition derives from the experiments of [S. G.] Soal," Stevenson writes. Eight years later it was discovered that Soal had cheated shamelessly on some of his tests, rendering all his research suspect.

My own skepticism about ESP is well known. I shall leave it to readers of this anthology as to whether the evidence for paranormal perception of the *Titanic* disaster is strong enough to support such an extraordinary claim or whether we have here the same familiar blend of unreliable anecdotes with coincidences of the sort that are well within the bounds of normal laws of chance.

As for the amazing mystique that has developed around the sinking of the *Titanic,* it is not hard to understand why it has been so long-lasting. It springs from the ironic juxtaposition of a titanic pride—the belief on the part of everyone concerned that this floating museum of conspicuous waste could not be sunk—and the unexpected suddenness with which that belief was shattered. Unlike so many other disasters, this one could easily have been prevented had there not been such a conflux of human errors. Like the fall of Babylon, the *Titanic's* sinking can be taken as a symbol of the crumbling of proud empires with their similar mix of the rich, the middle class, and the poor—all going down together. And now for the first time in history it can be taken as a symbol of the sudden fate of the entire human race if a combination of human follies should set off a nuclear war.

I wish to thank an old friend, Russell Barnhart, for assistance in researching several aspects of this book.

MARTIN GARDNER

Hendersonville, North Carolina

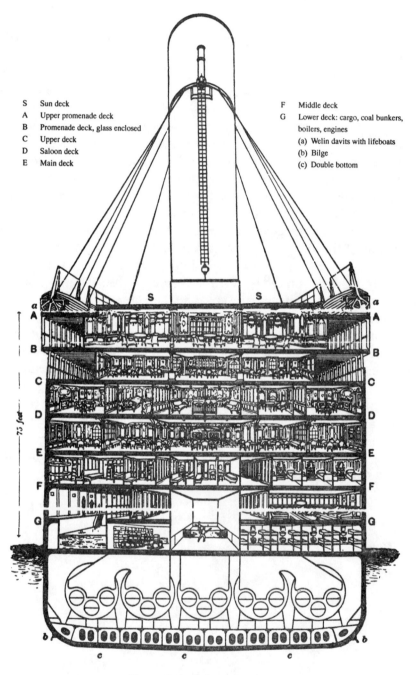

S Sun deck
A Upper promenade deck
B Promenade deck, glass enclosed
C Upper deck
D Saloon deck
E Main deck

F Middle deck
G Lower deck: cargo, coal bunkers,
  boilers, engines
 (a) Welin davits with lifeboats
 (b) Bilge
 (c) Double bottom

Cross-section of the *Titanic*

1

THE WRECK OF THE TITAN

MORGAN ROBERTSON

The single most impressive example of seeming precognition of the *Titanic* disaster, or any other disaster, is Morgan Robertson's short novel *Futility*. The 145 page book was first published by the New York firm of M. F. Mansfield in 1898, fourteen years before the *Titanic* sank. In 1912, *McClure's Magazine* reprinted it in the United States (and Bird, in London) under the title *The Wreck of the Titan; or, Futility*. The new book also included a longer novella by Robertson and two of his short stories.

I have chosen to reprint here the second version—the one Robertson obviously preferred. Copies of the 1898 edition are scarce, but it has been reprinted in full in two privately published books by Jack W. Hannah, a businessman in Mansfield, Ohio, using the firm name of the Didactic Publishing Company (Rural Route 3, Box 11, Mansfield, OH 44903). Mr. Hannah is an evangelical Protestant. *The Futility God: Spiritist Power, Occultism, and Futility,* his 1975 paperback, is mostly about theology. Hannah is firmly convinced that Robertson had the gift of prophecy and that his novel was divinely inspired—"a piece of literature that contains a word of God." This theme is expanded in his second paperback, a book of 520 pages, titled *The Titanic: Its Prophecy, Philosophy, and Psychology* (1980). Robertson made numerous revisions in *Futility* for its 1912 edition, but they are mostly changes of punctuation and phrasing and have almost no bearing on the story's prophetic aspects. As Hannah points out: if anything, the parallels are a trifle stronger in the 1898 version.

Before discussing the astounding similarities between the *Titanic* disaster and the sinking of Robertson's fictional ship, it will be worthwhile to summarize the *Titanic* story.

The R.M.S. *Titanic* was a White Star liner almost identical in size and structure to her older sister ship the *Olympic*. (The *Olympic* completed a maiden voyage to New York in May 1911.) On Wednesday,

April 10, 1912, the *Titanic* set sail from Southampton on her maiden voyage to New York. It was advertised as the largest, most elegant liner ever built. Moreover, this floating palace had been constructed in a way that was considered unsinkable. On board for the trip were some of the world's wealthiest people, including Mr. and Mrs. John Jacob Astor, Mr. and Mrs. Isidor Straus (he was cofounder of Macy's department store), Benjamin Guggenheim, Charles Hayes, president of a railway, and Bruce Ismay, chairman of the White Star Line.

Captain Edward J. Smith had been warned of icebergs, but he was eager to arrive in New York as soon as possible because the ship's return trip was supposed to begin on April 20. The night of Sunday, April 14, was clear and cold. There was no moon, but stars were bright and the sea calm. The captain increased the ship's speed to 22.5 knots, or 41.7 km an hour.

About 1,300 miles from New York, just before midnight, one of the six lookouts spotted an iceberg. The lookouts had not been provided with binoculars. If they had been, the accident might not have occurred. As it was, by the time Frederick Fleet, a 25-year-old seaman in the crow's nest, saw a dark mass and shouted "Iceberg right ahead!" it was too late to steer clear. The starboard side of the *Titanic* grazed the ice so smoothly that at first no one thought there had been any damage. Nobody panicked because everyone assumed the ship was unsinkable. Three hours later, on Monday, April 15, the *Titanic* sank in international waters. It came to rest under about 12,000 feet of ocean, where the pressure is two tons to a square inch. Not until September 1985 was the wreckage located and photographed. Whether the ship can be raised, or its compartments entered by specially built submarines, is not yet clear. Nor is it clear who owns whatever treasures can be salvaged.

When William Murdoch, the officer in command at the time the iceberg was spotted, heard the lookout's call, he instinctively ordered a reversal of engines and a "hard astarboard" to swing the bow of the ship to the port side. Everybody now agrees this was unwise, but experts differ on whether he should have ordered just a reversal of engines, keeping the course straight on the assumption that hitting the ice head on would have caused less damage, or whether he should have kept the hard starboard and *increased* the ship's speed to make it swerve faster. Apparently nothing could have been worse than combining hard starboard with reduced speed.

The *Californian,* a Leyland Line steamer, was only ten or twenty miles away at the time, but its wireless operator had gone to bed and so could not respond to the *Titanic*'s S.O.S. Even aside from this, as the British courts later brought out, the *Californian* could have come to the *Titanic*'s aid much earlier. Its sailors actually saw the ship's distress rockets, but the captain, when told about the rockets, refused to arouse his sleeping telegrapher. The captain didn't believe what his crew had told him.

The Cunard liner *Carpathia* was the first rescue ship on the scene, arriving an hour and twenty minutes after the *Titanic* had plunged bow foremost to the sea's bottom. The *Titanic* had an inadequate number of lifeboats, and the crew had not been trained on how to lower them because no one imagined they would ever be needed.

The precise number of lives lost is still not known, but more than 1,500 persons died, most of them immigrants in steerage. The White Star company was eventually absolved of negligence by the courts, though it paid heavy damages to many relatives of the dead. The accident led to stronger safety laws at sea, especially laws requiring more lifeboats and constant wireless watches.

Two prominent writers lost their lives in the disaster: W. T. Stead, about whom I shall say more in a later chapter, and Jacques Futrelle. Futrelle was an American journalist, age 37, who had written a series of popular mystery stories about a professor so adept at solving crimes that he was called "the thinking machine." Two collections of these stories had been published.

Many myths about the disaster were perpetuated in fiction and motion pictures. The ship's band did not play "Nearer My God to Thee" as the ship went down. It was probably a currently popular waltz called "Autumn." (Incidentally, none of the band's eight members survived.) There is no evidence that Captain Smith tried to kill himself or that he went down shouting, "Be British, boys, be British!" It is not known how he died. No man tried to get in a lifeboat dressed like a woman, although it is true that not everybody acted heroically and unselfishly.

The disaster produced a flood of books, stories, articles, songs, poems, and several motion pictures. Walter Lord's *A Night to Remember* (1955, revised 1976) has been the most popular of recent books. The latest and one of the best is Wyn Craig Wade's *The Titanic: End of a Dream* (1979).

There are two organizations of *Titanic* buffs, both in the United States. Each year on the anniversary of the disaster the Titanic Historical Society, headquartered at Indian Orchard, Massachusetts (Post Office Box 53), drops a wreath on the North Atlantic near the spot where the ship sank. The society also sponsors a dinner every five years and sells a variety of books and other publications, as well as such things as models of the *Titanic,* photographs, prints of paintings, post cards, jigsaw puzzles, slides, films, calendars, ship plans, and T-shirts that say "Remember the *Titanic.*"

A rival organization, the Oceanic Navigation Society, sponsors an annual *Titanic* Night every April. The front page of the *Wall Street Journal* (April 12, 1985) featured a long article about that year's *Titanic* Night in Los Angeles. About two hundred people paid $75 each for the occasion, danced to ragtime, and enjoyed a meal based on the *Titanic*'s First Class menu. Grim jokes circulated ("Heard what happened when Mrs. Astor sent for more ice?")—jokes that members of the more staid Titanic Historical Society consider in bad taste. Charles Sachs, a flamboyant character who heads the research society, told the *Journal* he was writing a play about Captain Smith and would like to sponsor an amusement park ride where people would climb into lifeboats on a small model of the *Titanic*. The ship would sink slowly and the boats would be rescued by a model of the *Carpathia*.

Morgan Andrew Robertson (1861-1915) was a popular American writer of romantic sea adventures. Born in Oswego, New York, the son of a Great Lakes ship captain, he joined the merchant service at 16, and for almost ten years his life on various ships gave him the material for his fiction. Robertson had no formal education beyond high school, but his ability to tell a fast-paced yarn made him one of the country's most widely read writers of sea stories. He wrote more than two hundred tales of varying length, most of which were reprinted in fourteen books.

In 1915, Robertson was found dead, standing up in a hotel room with his head resting on a bureau, after a heart attack. In 1915 *McClure's* published *Morgan Robertson the Man,* a collection of tributes by other writers, and his own short autobiography, "Gathering No Moss," first printed in the *Saturday Evening Post* (March 28, 1914). "I put in ten years before the mast," he begins his account. His final line: "I am a sailor!" The strangest aspect of this book is that nowhere does it mention the *Titanic* or Robertson's prophetic novel. Details of his sad life, which ended in destitution, are brought out, but not his lifelong problem of alcoholism. The entire book is reprinted in Jack Hannah's 1980 volume cited earlier.

One assumes that the many parallels between the wreck of Robertson's *Titan* and the sinking of the *Titanic* were responsible for changing the novel's title to *The Wreck of the Titan* when it was reprinted in 1912. Let us list the major parallels:

The *Titanic* was 882.5 feet long (about a sixth of a mile). The *Titan*, 800 feet.

Both ships were all steel, with three propellers and two masts.

Both ships were considered unsinkable because of their many water-tight compartments: 19 on the *Titan*, 16 on the *Titanic*. Both ships also had watertight doors: 92 on the *Titan*, 12 on the *Titanic*.

Each was called the largest passenger ship ever built.

Each could carry about 3,000 people. The *Titan* was filled to capacity. The *Titanic* carried 2,235.

The *Titanic* had a 66,000-ton displacement. The *Titan* was given 45,000 tons in the 1898 edition. In the 1912 revision it is 70,000 in Chapter 1, 75,000 in Chapter 7. Gross tonnage was 45,000 and 46,328, respectively.

The *Titanic*'s horse-power was 46,000. Robertson's *Titan* has 40,000 in his 1898 book (Chapter 1). This is inexplicably changed to 75,000 in the 1912 version.

Both ships had far too few lifeboats: 20 on the *Titanic*, 24 on the *Titan*.

The *Titanic* was going 22.5 knots when it hit the iceberg. The *Titan* was going 25 knots.

Both ships began their fatal voyage in April. No day of the month is specified in Robertson's novel.

Both struck an iceberg near midnight. It was a clear moonless night for the *Titanic*. The *Titan* was in moonlight and heavy fog.

Both ships grazed an iceberg on the starboard side.

Both ships were on the great circle connecting New York and England. The *Titanic* was making her maiden voyage from England to New York. The *Titan* was going the other way, and it was her third round-trip.

Both ships hit an iceberg at spots a few hundred miles apart.

Both ships were owned by a British firm headquartered in Liverpool, with a branch office on Broadway in Manhattan. The principal stock owners of both ships were American. As Hannah reports, in 1902 J. P. Morgan had obtained control of the White Star Line.

The outstanding difference between the two disasters was that in Robertson's story twice as many people died. About 1,520 *Titanic* passengers perished. Of the *Titan's* 3,000, only thirteen survived, including the captain and first mate.

These parallels, especially such similar names for the two ships, are so startling that it is easy to understand why Robertson's novel is so often hailed as paranormal foresight. In the 1970s a public hunger for sensational accounts of the paranormal were met by a large number of lurid hardcover books, swarming with sensational color pictures and breathless accounts of occult happenings. Grolier Enterprises led the way in the United States with no less than twenty-one such books in a series they called *The Library of the Supernatural*. The first volume, *Signs of Things to Come,* was heavily promoted by mail with a glossy four-page brochure accompanied by a "Dear friend . . ." letter signed by no less a psychic star than Uri Geller. Mitzi Bales edited this atrocious volume. The book's two consultants are listed as Geller and England's top purveyor of occult hogwash, Colin Wilson. The volume opens with five pages on the *Titanic*. There are pictures of the sinking liner and a drawing depicting an entirely mythical account of Captain Smith rescuing a baby. Much is made of the paranormal foresight of Robertson, incorrectly identified as a British writer.

The great success of this series, and others similar but worse, was not lost on the management of *Reader's Digest*. They got into the act with three sensational volumes, starting with *Strange Stories, Amazing Facts* (1976). In 1981 they topped all previous books on the occult with their 352-page *Into the Unknown,* edited by Will Bradbury, with sociologist Marcello Truzzi, of Eastern Michigan University, serving as consultant. Robertson's novel is discussed, along with W. E. Cox's study of premonitions of train wrecks and Ian Stevenson's papers on the *Titanic*. Not content with two shameless volumes, *Reader's Digest* produced their third monstrosity, *Mysteries of the Unexplained* (1983), edited by Carroll Calkins. It was promoted with a four-page foldout flyer even more sensational than the flyer for the previous volume. This book also covers Robertson's extrasensory perception of the *Titanic* tragedy.

Many occult journalists and low-level parapsychologists are convinced that Robertson, who had a strong personal interest in occult topics, experienced a paranormal vision of the *Titanic* disaster. Martin Ebon takes this view in his book *Prophecy in Our Time* (1968). So does Jule Eisenbud, psychiatrist, parapsychologist, and author of a notorious book about Ted Serios, a Chicago bellhop who convinced Eisenbud he could project images from his brain onto Polaroid film. Eisenbud's chapter on Robertson in his book *Paranormal Foreknowledge* (1982) is reprinted in his *Parapsychology and the Unconscious* (1983).

I earlier mentioned Hannah's privately printed books. Applying some dubious statistics—as Eisenbud points out, he neglects the fact that many of the *Titan-Titanic* parallels are not independent events—Hannah arrives at a probability estimate of 1 in 4 billion that the parallels could be chance coincidences! Eisenbud modifies this to 1 in 1,024, "hardly a prima facie basis for presuming that either chance or inference was involved."

How improbable were the parallels? This is impossible to answer because it is not a well-formed problem. There is no way to estimate, even crudely, the relevant probabilities. However, the parallels become less miraculous if you imagine yourself in Robertson's shoes at the time he wrote *Futility*. It is near the end of the century. You are a well-known writer of sea tales, and you have decided to weave an adventure around the greatest sea disaster you can imagine. How would you go about constructing the plot?

First of all you would invent the largest ocean liner that could be built at the time. As someone thoroughly familiar with the latest developments in shipbuilding you would envision a liner larger than any previously made, yet still within the capacity of the day's technology. By taking advantage of water-tight compartments and doors, and other features, the ship would be hailed as unsinkable. Such a belief would add irony and poignancy to your tragedy. What should you call your supership? *Titan* would certainly not be inappropriate.

You want the disaster to occur in peacetime. What could sink a monstrous liner except a monstrous iceberg? You know that every year small ships fatally collide with icebergs in the North Atlantic. There had already been disasters involving large liners. In 1856 the *Pacific* went down in a sea of icebergs. In 1879 the *Arizona* collided with an iceberg, though it managed to reach Iceland with a crumpled bow.

Similar collisions with icebergs would later crumple the bows of the *Concordia* (1907) and the *Columbia* (1911). Indeed, the danger of colliding with an iceberg was the most-feared event of a ship's crew when it crossed the North Atlantic. Stories had been written about such collisions, and newspaper editorials frequently warned that sooner or later such a wreck would be a major sea disaster. The time of greatest peril would be in early spring when the warm weather starts to melt polar ice, causing icebergs to detach and float south. Surely it is not surprising that the *Titan* and the *Titanic* each struck an iceberg in April.

Once you have decided on the features above as part of your plot, other details would jog into place—the ship's length, tonnage, carrying capacity, number of propellers, the claimed unsinkability, and so on. You know from years of experience at sea that damage to a ship is much greater when there is a side collision than when there is one straight on. As Robertson writes in Chapter 7: "Had the impact been received by a perpendicular wall, the elastic resistance of bending plates and frames would have overcome the momentum with no more damage to the passengers than a severe shaking up, and to the ship than the crushing in of her bows and the killing, to a man, of the watch below. She would have backed off, and, slightly down by the head, finished the voyage at reduced speed, to rebuild on insurance money, and benefit, largely, in the end, by the consequent advertising of her indestructibility."

Lifeboats? You want to stress in your novel the unbounded hubris that caused the ship's owners and officers to be careless, so of course you would give your ill-fated ship an inadequate supply of boats. Indeed, you would have almost all your passengers perish in contrast to what actually happened when the *Titanic* sank.

In fairness to Ian Stevenson, it must be said that in his first paper on the *Titanic* he made clear that in trying to evaluate the coincidences in *Futility* "we certainly cannot exclude inference as a source of Robertson's story":

At the end of the nineteenth century confidence in engineering skill ran high with few limits to its achievements discernible. The novels of Jules Verne and H. G. Wells predicted further extraordinary developments. That science has since outrun science fiction we all know. But we also know that the advance of engineering proceeds jerkily, the reach of science from time to time exceeding its grasp. Unanticipated obstacles arise, and these often bring disaster before new tactics finally master them. Such was the history of the first passenger jet airliners developed in Great Britain after the Second World War. And we may suppose that similar disasters will occur before the mastery of flight into outer space. A writer of the 1890's familiar with man's repeated *hubris* might reasonably infer that he would overreach himself in the construction of ocean liners which then, with skyscrapers and airplanes just beginning, were man's greatest engineering marvels. Granting then, a penetrating awareness of man's growing and excessive confidence in marine engineering, a thoughtful person might make additional inferences about the details of the tragedy to come. A large ship would probably have great power and speed; the name *Titan* has connoted power and security for several thousand years; overconfidence would neglect the importance of lifeboats; recklessness would race the ship through the areas of the Atlantic icebergs; these drift south in the spring, making April a likely month for collision.

Is it possible, many have asked, that whatever person or group was responsible for naming the *Titanic* may have been familiar with Robertson's story? His sea tales were certainly read in England and *Futility* had been published there in 1898. Could someone have recalled the *Titan* and proposed adding "ic" to the name? I suggest this as a research project for anyone interested in running down facts about how the *Titanic* got its name. However, as Hannah convincingly argues, it is difficult to imagine that anyone would want to name a big new liner after a fictional ship that went down when it hit an iceberg.

As always in trying to evaluate remarkable concidences we must remember to place them within the wider framework of combinatorial possibilities. It seems incredible, for example, that in Psalm 46 of the Bible the forty-sixth word is "shake" and the forty-sixth word from the end is "spear," and that Shakespeare was 46 when the King James translation was completed. Taken in isolation, such coincidences seem paranormal. But we must realize that in a book as vast as the Bible the probability is high that *some* astounding word coincidences would occur. It is like finding a long run of consecutive digits in the endless decimal expansion of pi. When thousands of stories are published about imaginary disasters—earthquakes, fires, floods, great battles, volcanic eruptions, tragic wrecks on land and sea and in the air—is it not likely that *some* will display astonishing parallels with actual disasters to come? Robertson's novel happens to be the best example we know of a "probable improbability" within the enormously large combinatorial universe of fictional possibilities.

As someone who enjoys finding coincidences in literature, I must confess that I squandered hours searching lists of *Titanic* passengers and crew for at least one last name that would match a name in Robertson's novel. To my surprise, I found none. The best I could do was the *Titan*'s Captain Bryce and a *Titanic* seaman name Brice. I also observed that Bryce and Smith, the *Titanic*'s captain, each spell with five letters. Perhaps some reader of this book, with a penchant for word play, can uncover less trivial examples.

Note how Robertson, in the last line of his revised novel, himself indulges in a bit of word play. The line is beautifully ambiguous. We do not know whether John Rowland, the novel's hero, is going to see Myra the daughter or Myra the mother. Incidentally, these last three paragraphs were not in *Futility*. Their addition is the only major change Robertson made. In the 1898 version the story ends with: "Now John Rowland, your future is your own. You have merely suffered in the past from a mistaken estimate of the importance of women and whisky."

The Wreck of the Titan

MORGAN ROBERTSON

Chapter I

She was the largest craft afloat and the greatest of the works of men.
In her construction and maintenance were involved every science,
profession, and trade known to civilization. On her bridge were
officers, who, besides being the pick of the Royal Navy, had passed
rigid examinations in all studies that pertained to the winds, tides,
currents, and geography of the sea; they were not only seamen, but
scientists. The same professional standard applied to the personnel of
the engine-room, and the stewards' department was equal to that of a
first-class hotel.

Two brass bands, two orchestras, and a theatrical company entertained the passengers during waking hours; a corps of physicians
attended to the temporal, and a corps of chaplains to the spiritual,
welfare of all on board, while a well-drilled fire-company soothed the
fears of nervous ones and added to the general entertainment by daily
practice with their apparatus.

From her lofty bridge ran hidden telegraph lines to the bow, stern
engine-room, crow's-nest on the foremast, and to all parts of the ship
where work was done, each wire terminating in a marked dial with a
movable indicator, containing in its scope every order and answer
required in handling the massive hulk, either at the dock or at sea—
which eliminated, to a great extent, the hoarse, nerve-racking shouts of
officers and sailors.

From the bridge, engine-room, and a dozen places on her deck the
ninety-two doors of nineteen watertight compartments could be closed
in half a minute by turning a lever. These doors would also close

37

automatically in the presence of water. With nine compartments flooded the ship would still float, and as no known accident of the sea could possibly fill this many, the steamship *Titan* was considered practically unsinkable.

Built of steel throughout, and for passenger traffic only, she carried no combustible cargo to threaten her destruction by fire; and the immunity from the demand for cargo space had enabled her designers to discard the flat, kettle-bottom of cargo boats and give her the sharp dead-rise—or slant from the keel—of a steam yacht, and this improved her behavior in a seaway. She was eight hundred feet long, of seventy thousand tons' displacement, seventy-five thousand horse-power, and on her trial trip had steamed at a rate of twenty-five knots an hour over the bottom, in the face of unconsidered winds, tides, and currents. In short, she was a floating city—containing within her steel walls all that tends to minimize the dangers and discomforts of the Atlantic voyage—all that makes life enjoyable.

Unsinkable—indestructible, she carried as few boats as would satisfy the laws. These, twenty-four in number, were securely covered and lashed down to their chocks on the upper deck, and if launched would hold five hundred people. She carried no useless, cumbersome life-rafts; but—because the law required it—each of the three thousand berths in the passengers', officers', and crews' quarters contained a cork jacket, while about twenty circular life-buoys were strewn along the rails.

In view of her absolute superiority to other craft, a rule of navigation thoroughly believed in by some captains, but not yet openly followed, was announced by the steamship company to apply to the *Titan:* She would steam at full speed in fog, storm, and sunshine, and on the Northern Lane Route, winter and summer, for the following good and substantial reasons: First, that if another craft should strike her, the force of the impact would be distributed over a larger area if the *Titan* had full headway, and the brunt of the damage would be borne by the other. Second, that if the *Titan* was the aggressor she would certainly destroy the other craft, even at half-speed, and perhaps damage her own bows; while at full speed, she would cut her in two with no more damage to herself than a paintbrush could remedy. In either case, as the lesser of two evils, it was best that the smaller hull should suffer. A third reason was that, at full speed, she could be more easily steered out of danger, and a fourth, that in case of an end-on collision with an iceberg—the only thing afloat that she could not conquer—her bows would be crushed in but a few feet further at full than at half speed, and at the most three compartments would be flooded—which would not matter with six more to spare.

So, it was confidently expected that when her engines had limbered themselves, the steamship *Titan* would land her passengers three thousand miles away with the promptitude and regularity of a railway train. She had beaten all records on her maiden voyage, but, up to the third return trip, had not lowered the time between Sandy Hook and Daunt's Rock to the five-day limit; and it was unofficially rumored among the two thousand passengers who had embarked at New York that an effort would now be made to do so.

Chapter II

Eight tugs dragged the great mass to midstream and pointed her nose down the river; then the pilot on the bridge spoke a word or two; the first officer blew a short blast on the whistle and turned a lever; the tugs gathered in their lines and drew off; down in the bowels of the ship three small engines were started, opening the throttles of three large ones; three propellers began to revolve; and the mammoth, with a vibratory tremble running through her great frame, moved slowly to sea.

East of Sandy Hook the pilot was dropped and the real voyage begun. Fifty feet below her deck, in an inferno of noise, and heat, and light, and shadow, coal-passers wheeled the picked fuel from the bunkers to the fire-hold, where half-naked stokers, with faces like those of tortured fiends, tossed it into the eighty white-hot mouths of the furnaces. In the engine-room, oilers passed to and fro, in and out of the plunging, twisting, glistening steel, with oil-cans and waste, overseen by the watchful staff on duty, who listened with strained hearing for a false note in the confused jumble of sound—a clicking of steel out of tune, which would indicate a loosened key or nut. On deck, sailors set the triangular sails on the two masts, to add their propulsion to the momentum of the record-breaker, and the passengers dispersed themselves as suited their several tastes. Some were seated in steamer chairs, well wrapped—for, though it was April, the salt air was chilly—some paced the deck, acquiring their sea legs; others listened to the orchestra in the music-room, or read or wrote in the library, and a few took to their berths—seasick from the slight heave of the ship on the ground-swell.

The decks were cleared, watches set at noon, and then began the never-ending cleaning-up at which steamship sailors put in so much of their time. Headed by a six-foot boatswain, a gang came aft on the starboard side, with paint-buckets and brushes, and distributed themselves along the rail.

"Davits an' stanchions, men—never mind the rail," said the boatswain. "Ladies, better move your chairs back a little. Rowland, climb down out o' that—you'll be overboard. Take a ventilator—no, you'll spill paint—put your bucket away an' get some sandpaper from the yeoman. Work inboard till you get it out o' you."

The sailor addressed—a slight-built man of about thirty, black-bearded and bronzed to the semblance of healthy vigor, but watery-eyed and unsteady of movement—came down from the rail and shambled forward with his bucket. As he reached the group of ladies to whom the boatswain had spoken, his gaze rested on one—a sunny-haired young woman with the blue of the sea in her eyes—who had arisen at his approach. He started, turned aside as if to avoid her, and raising his hand in an embarrassed half-salute, passed on. Out of the boatswain's sight he leaned against the deck-house and panted, while he held his hand to his breast.

"What is it?" he muttered, wearily: "whisky nerves, or the dying flutter of a starved love. Five years, now—and a look from her eyes can stop the blood in my veins—can bring back all the heart-hunger and helplessness, that leads a man to insanity—or this." He looked at his trembling hand, all scarred and tar-stained, passed on forward, and returned with the sandpaper.

The young woman had been equally affected by the meeting. An expression of mingled surprise and terror had come to her pretty, but rather weak face; and without acknowledging his half-salute, she had caught up a little child from the deck behind her, and turning into the saloon door, hurried to the library, where she sank into a chair beside a military-looking gentleman, who glanced up from a book and remarked: "Seen the sea-serpent, Myra, or the Flying Dutchman? What's up?"

"Oh, George—no," she answered in agitated tones. "John Rowland is here—Lieutenant Rowland. I've just seen him—he is so changed—he tried to speak to me."

"Who—that troublesome flame of yours? I never met him, you know, and you haven't told me much about him. What is he—first cabin?"

"No, he seems to be a common sailor; he is working, and is dressed in old clothes—all dirty. And such a dissipated face, too. He seems to have fallen—so low. And it is all since—"

"Since you soured on him? Well, it is no fault of yours, dear. If a man has it in him he'll go to the dogs anyhow. How is his sense of injury? Has he a grievance or a grudge? You're badly upset. What did he say?"

"I don't know—he said nothing—I've always been afraid of him. I've met him three times since then, and he puts such a frightful look in his eyes—and he was so violent, and headstrong, and so terribly angry,—that time. He accused me of leading him on, and playing with him; and he said something about an immutable law of chance, and a governing balance of events—that I couldn't understand, only where he said that for all the suffering we inflict on others, we receive an equal amount ourselves. Then he went away—in such a passion. I've imagined ever since that he would take some revenge—he might steal our Myra—our baby." She strained the smiling child to her breast and went on. "I liked him at first, until I found out that he was an atheist—why, George, he actually denied the existence of God—and to me, a professing Christian."

"He had a wonderful nerve," said the husband, with a smile; "didn't know you very well, I should say."

"He never seemed the same to me after that," she resumed; "I felt as though in the presence of something unclean. Yet I thought how glorious it would be if I could save him to God, and tried to convince him of the loving care of Jesus; but he only ridiculed all I hold sacred, and said, that much as he valued my good opinion, he would not be a hypocrite to gain it, and that he would be honest with himself and others, and express his honest unbelief—the idea; as though one could be honest without God's help—and then, one day, I smelled liquor on his breath—he always smelled of tobacco—and I gave him up. It was then that he—that he broke out."

"Come out and show me this reprobate," said the husband, rising. They went to the door and the young woman peered out. "He is the last man down there—close to the cabin," she said as she drew in. The husband stepped out.

"What! that hang-dog ruffian, scouring the ventilator? So, that's Rowland, of the navy, is it! Well, this is a tumble. Wasn't he broken for conduct unbecoming an officer? Got roaring drunk at the President's levee, didn't he? I think I read of it."

"I know he lost his position and was terribly disgraced," answered his wife.

"Well, Myra, the poor devil is harmless now. We'll be across in a few days, and you needn't meet him on this broad deck. If he hasn't lost all sensibility, he's as embarrassed as you. Better stay in now—it's getting foggy."

Chapter III

When the watch turned out at midnight, they found a vicious half-gale blowing from the northeast, which, added to the speed of the steam-ship, made, so far as effects on her deck went, a fairly uncomfortable whole gale of chilly wind. The head sea, choppy as compared with her great length, dealt the *Titan* successive blows, each one attended by supplementary tremors to the continuous vibrations of the engines— each one sending a cloud of thick spray aloft that reached the crow's-nest on the foremast and battered the pilot-house windows on the bridge in a liquid bombardment that would have broken ordinary glass. A fog-bank, into which the ship had plunged in the afternoon, still enveloped her—damp and impenetrable; and into the gray, ever-receding wall ahead, with two deck officers and three lookouts straining sight and hearing to the utmost, the great racer was charging with undiminished speed.

At a quarter past twelve, two men crawled in from the darkness at the ends of the eighty-foot bridge and shouted to the first officer, who had just taken the deck, the names of the men who had relieved them. Backing up to the pilot-house, the officer repeated the names to a quatermaster within, who entered them in the log-book. Then the men vanished—to their coffee and "watch-below." In a few moments another dripping shape appeared on the bridge and reported the crow's-nest relief.

"Rowland, you say?" bawled the officer above the howling of the wind. "Is he the man who was lifted aboard, drunk, yesterday?"

"Yes, sir."

"Is he still drunk?"

"Yes, sir."

"All right—that'll do. Enter Rowland in the crow's-nest, quartermaster," said the officer; then, making a funnel of his hands, he roared out: "Crow's-nest, there."

"Sir," came the answer, shrill and clear on the gale.

"Keep your eyes open—keep a sharp lookout."

"Very good, sir."

"Been a man-o'-war's-man, I judge, by his answer. They're no good," muttered the officer. He resumed his position at the forward side of the bridge where the wooden railing afforded some shelter from the raw wind, and began the long vigil which would only end when the second officer relieved him, four hours later. Conversation—except in the line of duty—was forbidden among the bridge officers of the *Titan,* and his watchmate, the third officer, stood on the other side of the large bridge binnacle, only leaving this position occasionally to glance in at the compass—which seemed to be his sole duty at sea. Sheltered by one of the deck-houses below, the boatswain and the watch paced back and forth, enjoying the only two hours respite which steamship rules afforded, for the day's work had ended with the going down of the other watch, and at two o'clock the washing of the 'tween-deck would begin, as an opening task in the next day's labor.

By the time one bell had sounded, with its repetition from the crow's-nest, followed by a long-drawn cry—"all's well"—from the lookouts, the last of the two thousand passengers had retired, leaving the spacious cabins and steerage in possession of the watchmen; while, sound asleep in his cabin abaft the chart-room was the captain, the commander who never commanded—unless the ship was in danger; for the pilot had charge, making and leaving port, and the officers, at sea.

Two bells were struck and answered; then three, and the boatswain and his men were lighting up for a final smoke, when there rang out overhead a startling cry from the crow's-nest:

"Something ahead, sir—can't make it out."

The first officer sprang to the engine-room telegraph and grasped the lever. "Sing out what you see, " he roared.

"Hard aport, sir—ship on the starboard tack—dead ahead," came the cry.

"Port your wheel—hard over," repeated the first officer to the quartermaster at the helm—who answered and obeyed. Nothing as yet could be seen from the bridge. The powerful steering-engine in the stern ground the rudder over; but before three degrees on the compass card were traversed by the lubber's-point, a seeming thickening of the darkness and fog ahead resolved itself into the square sails of a deep-laden ship, crossing the *Titan's* bow, not half her length away.

"H—l and d———" growled the first officer. "Steady on your course, quartermaster," he shouted. "Stand from under on deck." He turned a lever which closed compartments, pushed a button marked—"Captain's Room," and crouched down, awaiting the crash.

There was hardly a crash. A slight jar shook the forward end of the *Titan* and sliding down her foretopmast-stay and rattling on deck came a shower of small spars, sails, blocks, and wire rope. Then, in the darkness to starboard and port, two darker shapes shot by—the two halves of the ship she had cut through; and from one of these shapes, where still burned a binnacle light, was heard, high above the confused murmur of shouts and shrieks, a sailorly voice:

"May the curse of God light on you and your cheese-knife, you brass-bound murderers."

The shapes were swallowed in the blackness astern; the cries were hushed by the clamor of the gale, and the steamship *Titan* swung back to her course. The first officer had not turned the lever of the engine-room telegraph.

The boatswain bounded up the steps of the bridge for instructions.

"Put men at the hatches and doors. Send every one who comes on deck to the chart-room. Tell the watchman to notice what the passengers have learned, and clear away that wreck forward as soon as possible." The voice of the officer was hoarse and strained as he gave these directions, and the "aye, aye, sir" of the boatswain was uttered in a gasp.

Chapter IV

The crow's-nest "look-out," sixty feet above the deck, had seen every detail of the horror, from the moment when the upper sails of the doomed ship had appeared to him above the fog to the time when the last tangle of wreckage was cut away by his watchmates below. When relieved at four bells, he descended with as little strength in his limbs as was compatible with safety in the rigging. At the rail, the boatswain met him.

"Report your relief, Rowland," he said, "and go into the chart-room!"

On the bridge, as he gave the name of his successor, the first officer seized his hand, pressed it, and repeated the boatswain's order. In the chart-room, he found the captain of the *Titan,* pale-faced and intense in manner, seated at a table, and, grouped around him, the whole of the watch on deck except the officers, lookouts, and quarter-masters. The cabin watchmen were there, and some of the watch below, among whom were stokers and coal-passers, and also, a few of the idlers—lampmen, yeomen, and butchers, who, sleeping forward, had been awakened by the terrific blow of the great hollow knife within which they lived.

Three carpenters' mates stood by the door, with sounding-rods in their hands, which they had just shown the captain—dry. Every face, from the captain's down, wore a look of horror and expectancy. A quartermaster followed Rowland in and said:

"Engineer felt no jar in the engine-room, sir; and there's no excitement in the stokehold."

"And you watchmen report no alarm in the cabins. How about the steerage? Is that man back?" asked the captain. Another watchman appeared as he spoke.

"All asleep in the steerage, sir," he said. Then a quartermaster entered with the same report of the forecastles.

"Very well," said the captain, rising; "one by one come into my office—watchmen first, then petty officers, then the men. Quarter-masters will watch the door—that no man goes out until I have seen him." He passed into another room, followed by a watchman, who presently emerged and went on deck with a more pleasant expression of face. Another entered and came out; then another, and another, until every man but Rowland had been within the sacred precincts, all to wear the same pleased, or satisfied, look on reappearing. When Rowland entered, the captain, seated at a desk, motioned him to a chair, and asked his name.

"John Rowland," he answered. The captain wrote it down.

"I understand," he said, "that you were in the crow's-nest when this unfortunate collision occurred."

"Yes, sir; and I reported the ship as soon as I saw her."

"You are not here to be censured. You are aware, of course, that nothing could be done, either to avert this terrible calamity, or to save life afterward."

"Nothing at a speed of twenty-five knots an hour in a thick fog, sir." The captain glanced sharply at Rowland and frowned.

"We will not discuss the speed of the ship, my good man," he said, "or the rules of the company. You will find, when you are paid at Liverpool, a package addressed to you at the company's office containing one hundred pounds in banknotes. This, you will receive for your silence in regard to this collision—the reporting of which would embarrass the company and help no one."

"On the contrary, captain, I shall not receive it. On the contrary, sir, I shall speak of this wholesale murder at the first opportunity!"

The captain leaned back and stared at the debauched face, the trembling figure of the sailor, with which this defiant speech so little accorded. Under ordinary circumstances, he would have sent him on deck to be dealt with by the officers. But this was not an ordinary circumstance. In the watery eyes was a look of shock, and horror, and honest indignation; the accents were those of an educated man; and the consequences hanging over himself and the company for which he worked—already complicated by and involved in his efforts to avoid them—which this man might precipitate, were so extreme, that such questions as insolence and difference in rank were not to be thought of. He must meet and subdue this Tartar on common ground—as man to man.

"Are you aware, Rowland," he asked, quietly, "that you will stand alone—that you will be discredited, lose your berth, and make enemies?"

"I am aware of more than that," answered Rowland, excitedly. "I know of the power vested in you as captain. I know that you can order me into irons from this room for any offense you wish to imagine. And I know that an unwitnessed, uncorroborated entry in your official log concerning me would be evidence enough to bring me life imprisonment. But I also know something of admiralty law; that from my prison cell I can send you and your first officer to the gallows."

"You are mistaken in your conceptions of evidence. I could not cause your conviction by a logbook entry; nor could you, from a prison, injure me. What are you, may I ask—an ex-lawyer?"

"A graduate of Annapolis. Your equal in professional technic."

"And you have interest at Washington?"

"None whatever."

"And what is your object in taking this stand—which can do you no possible good, though certainly not the harm you speak of?"

"That I may do one good, strong act in my useless life—that I may help to arouse such a sentiment of anger in the two countries as will forever end this wanton destruction of life and property for the sake of speed—that will save the hundreds of fishing-craft, and others, run down yearly, to their owners, and the crews to their families."

Both men had risen and the captain was pacing the floor as Rowland, with flashing eyes and clinched fists, delivered this declaration.

"A result to be hoped for, Rowland," said the former, pausing before him, "but beyond your power or mine to accomplish. Is the amount I named large enough? Could you fill a position on my bridge?"

"I can fill a higher; and your company is not rich enough to buy me."

"You seem to be a man without ambition; but you must have wants."

"Food, clothing, shelter—and whisky," said Rowland with a bitter, self-contemptuous laugh. The captain reached down a decanter and two glasses from a swinging tray and said as he placed them before him:

"Here is one of your wants; fill up," Rowland's eyes glistened as he poured out a glassful, and the captain followed.

"I will drink with you, Rowland," he said; "here is to our better understanding." He tossed off the liquor; then Rowland, who had waited, said: "I prefer drinking alone, captain," and drank the whisky at a gulp. The captain's face flushed at the affront, but he controlled himself.

"Go on deck, now, Rowland," he said; "I will talk with you again before we reach soundings. Meanwhile, I request—not require, but request—that you hold no useless conversation with your shipmates in regard to this matter."

To this first officer, when relieved at eight bells, the captain said: "He is a broken-down wreck with a temporarily active conscience; but is not the man to buy or intimidate: he knows too much. However, we've found his weak point. If he gets snakes before we dock, his testimony is worthless. Fill him up and I'll see the surgeon, and study up on drugs."

When Rowland turned out to breakfast at seven bells that morning, he found a pint flask in the pocket of his pea-jacket, which he felt of but did not pull out in sight of his watchmates.

"Well, captain," he thought, "you are, in truth, about as puerile, insipid a scoundrel as ever escaped the law. I'll save you your drugged Dutch courage for evidence." But it was not drugged, as he learned later. It was good whisky—a leader—to warm his stomach while the captain was studying.

Chapter V

An incident occurred that morning which drew Rowland's thought far from the happenings of the night. A few hours of bright sunshine had brought the passengers on deck like bees from a hive, and the two broad promenades resembled, in color and life, the streets of a city. The watch was busy at the inevitable scrubbing, and Rowland, with a swab and bucket, was cleaning the white paint on the starboard taffrail, screened from view by the after deck-house, which shut off a narrow space at the stern. A little girl ran into the inclosure, laughing and screaming, and clung to his legs, while she jumped up and down in an overflow of spirits.

"I wunned 'way," she said; "I wunned 'way from mamma."

Drying his wet hands on his trousers, Rowland lifted the tot and said, tenderly: "Well, little one, you must run back to mamma. You're in bad company." The innocent eyes smiled into his own, and then—a foolish proceeding, which only bachelors are guilty of—he held her above the rail in jesting menace. "Shall I drop you over to the fishes, baby?" he asked, while his features softened to an unwonted smile. The child gave a little scream of fright, and at that instant a young woman appeared around the corner. She sprang toward Rowland like a tigress, snatched the child, stared at him for a moment with dilated eyes, and then disappeared, leaving him limp and nerveless, breathing hard.

"It is her child," he groaned. "That was the mother-look. She is married—married." He resumed his work, with a face as near the color of the paint he was scrubbing as the tanned skin of a sailor may become.

Ten minutes later, the captain, in his office, was listening to a complaint from a very excited man and woman.

"And you say, colonel," said the captain, "that this man Rowland is an old enemy?"

"He is—or was once—a rejected admirer of Mrs. Selfridge. That is all I know of him—except that he has hinted at revenge. My wife is certain of what she saw, and I think the man should be confined."

"Why, captain," said the woman, vehemently, as she hugged her child, "you should have seen him; he was just about to drop Myra over as I seized her—and he had such a frightful leer on his face, too. Oh, it was hideous. I shall not sleep another wink in this ship—I know."

"I beg you will give yourself no uneasiness, madam," said the captain, gravely. "I have already learned something of his antecedents— that he is a disgraced and broken-down naval officer; but, as he has sailed three voyages with us, I had credited his willingness to work before-the-mast to his craving for liquor, which he could not satisfy without money. However—as you think—he may be following you. Was he able to learn of your movements—that you were to take passage in this ship?"

"Why not?" exclaimed the husband; "he must know some of Mrs. Selfridge's friends."

"Yes, yes," she said, eagerly; "I have heard him spoken of, several times."

"Then it is clear," said the captain. "If you will agree, madam, to testify against him in the English courts, I will immediately put him in irons for attempted murder."

"Oh, do, captain," she exclaimed. "I cannot feel safe while he is at liberty. Of course I will testify."

"Whatever you do, captain," said the husband, savagely, "rest assured that I shall put a bullet through his head if he meddles with me or mine again. Then you can put me in irons."

"I will see that he is attended to, colonel," replied the captain as he bowed them out of his office.

But, as a murder charge is not always the best way to discredit a man; and as the captain did not believe that the man who had defied him would murder a child; and as the charge would be difficult to prove in any case, and would cause him much trouble and annoyance, he did not order the arrest of John Rowland, but merely directed that, for the time, he should be kept at work by day in the 'tween-deck, out of sight of the passengers.

Rowland, surprised at his sudden transfer from the disagreeable scrubbing to a "soldier's job" of painting life-buoys in the warm 'tween-deck, was shrewd enough to know that he was being closely watched by the boatswain that morning, but not shrewd enough to affect any symptoms of intoxication or drugging, which might have satisfied his anxious superiors and brought him more whisky. As a result of his brighter eyes and steadier voice—due to the curative sea air—when he turned out for the first dog-watch on deck at four o'clock, the captain and boatswain held an interview in the chart-room, in which the former said: "Do not be alarmed. It is not poison. He is half-way into the horrors now, and this will merely bring them on. He will see snakes, ghosts, goblins, shipwrecks, fire, and all sorts of things. It works in two or three hours. Just drop it into his drinking pot while the port forecastle is empty."

There was a fight in the port forecastle—to which Rowland belonged—at supper time, which need not be described beyond mention of the fact that Rowland, who was not a participant, had his pot of tea dashed from his hand before he had taken three swallows. He procured a fresh supply and finished his supper; then, taking no part in his watchmates' open discussion of the fight, and guarded discussion of collisions, rolled into his bunk and smoked until eight bells, when he turned out with the rest.

Chapter VI

"Rowland," said the big boatswain, as the watch mustered on deck; "take the starboard bridge lookout."

"It is not my trick, boats'n," said Rowland, in surprise.

"Orders from the bridge. Get up there."

Rowland grumbled, as sailors may when aggrieved, and obeyed.

The man he relieved reported his name, and disappeared; the first officer sauntered down the bridge, uttered the official, "keep a good lookout," and returned to his post; then the silence and loneliness of a night-watch at sea, intensified by the never-ceasing hum of the engines, and relieved only by the sounds of distant music and laughter from the theater, descended on the forward part of the ship. For the fresh westerly wind, coming with the *Titan*, made nearly a calm on her deck; and the dense fog, though overshone by a bright star-specked sky, was so chilly that the last talkative passenger had fled to the light and life within.

When three bells—half-past nine—had sounded, and Rowland had given in his turn the required call—"all's well"—the first officer left his post and approached him.

"Rowland," he said as he drew near; "I hear you've walked the quarter-deck."

"I cannot imagine how you learned it, sir," replied Rowland; "I am not in the habit of referring to it."

"You told the captain. I suppose the curriculum is as complete at Annapolis as at the Royal Naval College. What do you think of Maury's theories of currents?"

"They seem plausible," said Rowland, unconsciously dropping the "sir"; "but I think that in most particulars he has been proven wrong."

"Yes, I think so myself. Did you ever follow up another idea of his—that of locating the position of ice in a fog by the rate of decrease in temperature as approached?"

"Not to any definite result. But it seems to be only a matter of calculation, and time to calculate. Cold is negative heat, and can be treated like radiant energy, decreasing as the square of the distance."

The officer stood a moment, looking ahead and humming a tune to himself; then, saying: "Yes, that's so," returned to his place.

"Must have a cast-iron stomach," he muttered, as he peered into the binnacle; "or else the boats'n dosed the wrong man's pot."

Rowland glanced after the retreating officer with a cynical smile. "I wonder," he said to himself, "why he comes down here talking navigation to a foremast hand. Why am I up here—out of my turn? Is this something in line with that bottle?" He resumed the short pacing back and forth on the end of the bridge, and the rather gloomy train of thought which the officer had interrupted.

"How long," he mused, "would his ambition and love of profession last him after he had met, and won, and lost, the only woman on earth to him? Why is it—that failure to hold the affections of one among the millions of women who live, and love, can outweigh every blessing in life, and turn a man's nature into a hell, to consume him? Who did she marry? Some one, probably a stranger long after my banishment, who came to her possessed of a few qualities of mind or physique that pleased her,—who did not need to love her—his chances were better without that—and he steps coolly and easily into my heaven. And they tell us, that 'God doeth all things well,' and that there is a heaven where all our unsatisfied wants are attended to—provided we have the necessary faith in it. That means, if it means anything, that after a lifetime of unrecognized allegiance, during which I win nothing but her fear and contempt, I may be rewarded by the love and companionship of her soul. Do I love her soul? Has her soul beauty of face and the figure and carriage of a Venus? Has her soul deep, blue eyes and a sweet, musical voice? Has it wit, and grace, and charm? Has it a wealth of pity for suffering? These are the things I loved. I do not love her soul, if she has one. I do not want it. I want her—I need her." He stopped in his walk and leaned against the bridge railing, with eyes fixed on the fog ahead. He was speaking his thoughts aloud now, and the first officer drew within hearing, listened a moment, and went back. "Working on him," he whispered to the third officer. Then he pushed the button which called the captain, blew a short blast of the steam whistle as a call to the boatswain, and resumed his watch on the drugged lookout, while the third officer conned the ship.

The steam call to the boatswain is so common a sound on a steamship as to generally pass unnoticed. This call affected another besides the boatswain. A little night-gowned figure arose from an under berth in a saloon stateroom, and, with wide-open, staring eyes, groped its way to the deck, unobserved by the watchman. The white, bare little feet felt no cold as they pattered the planks of the deserted promenade, and the little figure had reached the steerage entrance by the time the captain and boatswain had reached the bridge.

"And they talk," went on Rowland, as the three watched and listened; "of the wonderful love and care of a merciful God, who controls all things—who has given me my defects, and my capacity for loving, and then placed Myra Gaunt in my way. Is there mercy to me in this? As part of a great evolutionary principle, which develops the race life at the expense of the individual, it might be consistent with the idea of a God—a first cause. But does the individual who perishes, because unfitted to survive, owe any love, or gratitude to this God? He does not! On the supposition that He exists, I deny it! And on the complete lack of evidence that He does exist, I affirm to myself the integrity of cause and effect—which is enough to explain the Universe, and me. A merciful God—a kind, loving, just, and merciful God—" he burst into a fit of incongruous laughter, which stopped short as he clapped his hands to his stomach and then to his head. "What ails me?" he gasped; "I feel as though I had swallowed hot coals—and my head—and my eyes—I can't see." The pain left him in a moment and the laughter returned. "What's wrong with the starboard anchor? It's moving. It's changing. It's a—what? What on earth is it? On end—and the windlass—and the spare anchors—and the davits—all alive—all moving."

The sight he saw would have been horrid to a healthy mind, but it only moved this man to increased and uncontrollable merriment. The two rails below leading to the stem had arisen before him in a shadowy triangle; and within it were the deck-fittings he had mentioned. The windlass had become a thing of horror, black and forbidding. The two end barrels were the bulging, lightless eyes of a nondescript monster, for which the cable chains had multiplied themselves into innumerable legs and tentacles. And this thing was crawling around within the triangle. The anchor-davits were many-headed serpents which danced on their tails, and the anchors themselves writhed and squirmed in the shape of immense hairy caterpillars, while faces appeared on the two white lantern-towers—grinning and leering at him. With his hands on the bridge rail, and tears streaming down his face, he laughed at the strange sight, but did not speak; and the three, who had quietly approached, drew back to await, while below on the promenade deck, the little white figure, as though attracted by his laughter, turned into the stairway leading to the upper deck.

The phantasmagoria faded to a blank wall of gray fog, and Rowland found sanity to mutter, "They've drugged me"; but in an instant he stood in the darkness of a garden—one that he had known. In the distance were the lights of a house, and close to him was a young girl, who turned from him and fled, even as he called to her.

By a supreme effort of will, he brought himself back to the present, to the bridge he stood upon, and to his duty. "Why must it haunt me through the years," he groaned; "drunk then—drunk since. She could have saved me, but she chose to damn me." He strove to pace up and down, but staggered, and clung to the rail; while the three watchers approached again, and the little white figure below climbed the upper bridge steps.

"The survival of the fittest," he rambled, as he stared into the fog; "cause and effect. It explains the Universe—and me." He lifted his hand and spoke loudly, as though to some unseen familiar of the deep. "What will be the last effect? Where in the scheme of ultimate balance—under the law of the correlation of energy, will my wasted wealth of love be gathered, and weighed, and credited? What will balance it, and where will I be? Myra,—Myra," he called; "do you know what you have lost? Do you know, in your goodness, and purity, and truth, of what you have done? Do you know—"

The fabric on which he stood was gone, and he seemed to be poised on nothing in a worldless universe of gray—alone. And in the vast, limitless emptiness there was no sound, or life, or change; and in his heart neither fear, nor wonder, nor emotion of any kind, save one—the unspeakable hunger of a love that had failed. Yet it seemed that he was not John Rowland, but some one, or something else; for presently he saw himself, far away—millions of billions of miles; as though on the outermost fringes of the void—and heard his own voice, calling. Faintly, yet distinctly, filled with the concentrated despair of his life, came the call: "Myra—Myra."

There was an answering call, and looking for the second voice, he beheld her—the woman of his love—on the opposite edge of space; and her eyes held the tenderness, and her voice held the pleading that he had known but in dreams. "Come back," she called; "come back to me." But it seemed that the two could not understand; for again he heard the despairing cry: "Myra, Myra, where are you?" and again the answer: "Come back. Come."

Then in the far distance to the right appeared a faint point of flame, which grew larger. It was approaching, and he dispassionately viewed it; and when he looked again for the two, they were gone, and in their places were two clouds of nebula, which resolved into myriad points of sparkling light and color—whirling, encroaching, until they filled all space. And through them the larger light was coming—and growing larger—straight for him.

He heard a rushing sound, and looking for it, saw in the opposite direction a formless object, as much darker than the gray of the void as the flame was brighter, and it too was growing larger, and coming. And it seemed to him that this light and darkness were the good and evil of his life, and he watched, to see which would reach him first, but felt no surprise or regret when he saw that the darkness was nearest. It came, closer and closer, until it brushed him on the side.

"What have we here, Rowland?" said a voice. Instantly, the whirling points were blotted out; the universe of gray changed to the fog; the flame of light to the moon rising above it, and the shapeless darkness to the form of the first officer. The little white figure, which had just darted past the three watchers, stood at his feet. As though warned by an inner subconsciousness of danger, it had come in its sleep, for safety and care, to its mother's old lover—the strong and the weak—the degraded and disgraced, but exalted—the persecuted, drugged, and all but helpless John Rowland.

With the readiness with which a man who dozes while standing will answer the question that wakens him, he said—though he stammered from the now waning effect of the drug: "Myra's child, sir; it's asleep." He picked up the night-gowned little girl, who screamed as she wakened, and folded his pea-jacket around the cold little body.

"Who is Myra?" asked the officer in a bullying tone, in which were also chagrin and disappointment. "You've been asleep yourself."

Before Rowland could reply a shout from the crow's-nest split the air.

"Ice," yelled the lookout: "ice ahead. Iceberg. Right under the bows." The first officer ran amidships, and the captain, who had remained there, sprang to the engine-room telegraph, and this time the lever was turned. But in five seconds the bow of the *Titan* began to lift, and ahead, and on either hand, could be seen, through the fog, a field of ice, which arose in an incline to a hundred feet high in her track. The music in the theater ceased, and among the babel of shouts and cries, and the deafening noise of steel, scraping and crashing over ice, Rowland heard the agonized voice of a woman crying from the bridge steps: "Myra—Myra, where are you? Come back."

Chapter VII

Seventy-five thousand tons—dead-weight—rushing through the fog at the rate of fifty feet a second, had hurled itself at an iceberg. Had the impact been received by a perpendicular wall, the elastic resistance of bending plates and frames would have overcome the momentum with no more damage to the passengers than a severe shaking up, and to the ship than the crushing in of her bows and the killing, to a man, of the watch below. She would have backed off, and, slightly down by the head, finished the voyage at reduced speed, to rebuild on insurance money, and benefit, largely, in the end, by the consequent advertising of her indestructibility. But a low beach, possibly formed by the recent overturning of the berg, received the *Titan,* and with her keel cutting the ice like the steel runner of an iceboat, and her great weight resting on the starboard bilge, she rose out of the sea, higher and higher—until the propellers in the stern were half exposed—then, meeting an easy spiral rise in the ice under her port bow, she heeled, overbalanced, and crashed down on her side, to starboard.

The holding-down bolts of twelve boilers and three triple-expansion engines, unintended to hold such weights from a perpendicular flooring, snapped, and down through a maze of ladders, gratings, and fore-and-aft bulkheads came these giant masses of steel and iron, puncturing the sides of the ship, even where backed by solid, resisting ice; and filling the engine- and boiler-rooms with scalding steam, which brought a quick, though tortured death, to each of the hundred men on duty in the engineer's department.

Amid the roar of escaping steam, and the bee-like buzzing of nearly three thousand human voices, raised in agonized screams and callings from within the inclosing walls, and the whistling of air through hundreds of open dead-lights as the water, entering the holes of the crushed and riven starboard side, expelled it, the *Titan* moved slowly backward and launched herself into the sea, where she floated low on her side—a dying monster, groaning with her death-wound.

A solid, pyramid-like hummock of ice, left to starboard as the steamer ascended, and which projected close alongside the upper, or boat-deck, as she fell over, had caught, in succession, every pair of davits to starboard, bending and wrenching them, smashing boats, and snapping tackles and gripes, until, as the ship cleared herself, it capped the pile of wreckage strewing the ice in front of, and around it, with the end and broken stanchions of the bridge. And in this shattered, box-like structure, dazed by the sweeping fall through an arc of seventy-foot radius, crouched Rowland, bleeding from a cut in his head, and still holding to his breast the little girl—now too frightened to cry.

By an effort of will, he aroused himself and looked. To his eyesight, twisted and fixed to a shorter focus by the drug he had taken, the steamship was little more than a bloth on the moon-whitened fog; yet he thought he could see men clambering and working on the upper davits, and the nearest boat—No. 24—seemed to be swinging by the tackles. Then the fog shut her out, though her position was still indicated by the roaring of steam from her iron lungs. This ceased in time, leaving behind it the horrid humming sound and whistling of air; and when this too was suddenly hushed, and the ensuing silence broken by dull, booming reports—as from bursting compartments—Rowland knew that the holocaust was complete; that the invincible *Titan,* with nearly all of her people, unable to climb vertical floors and ceilings, was beneath the surface of the sea.

Mechanically, his benumbed faculties had received and recorded the impressions of the last few moments; he could not comprehend, to the full, the horror of it all. Yet his mind was keenly alive to the peril of the woman whose appealing voice he had heard and recognized—the woman of his dream, and the mother of the child in his arms. He hastily examined the wreckage. Not a boat was intact. Creeping down to the water's edge, he hailed, with all the power of his weak voice, to possible, but invisible boats beyond the fog—calling on them to come and save the child—to look out for a woman who had been on deck, under the bridge. He shouted this woman's name—the one that he knew—encouraging her to swim, to tread water, to float on wreckage, and to answer him, until he came to her. There was no response, and when his voice had grown hoarse and futile, and his feet numb from the cold of the thawing ice, he returned to the wreckage, weighed down and all but crushed by the blackest desolation that had, so far, come into his unhappy life. The little girl was crying and he tried to soothe her.

"I want mamma," she wailed.

"Hush, baby, hush," he answered, wearily and bitterly; "so do I—more than Heaven, but I think our chances are about even now. Are you cold, little one? We'll go inside, and I'll make a house for us."

He removed his coat, tenderly wrapped the little figure in it, and with the injunction: "Don't be afraid, now," placed her in the corner of the bridge, which rested on its forward side. As he did so, the bottle of whisky fell out of the pocket. It seemed an age since he had found it there, and it required a strong effort of reasoning before he remembered its full significance. Then he raised it, to hurl it down the incline of ice, but stopped himself.

"I'll keep it," he muttered; "it may be safe in small quantities, and we'll need it on this ice." He placed it in a corner; then, removing the canvas cover from one of the wrecked boats, he hung it over the open side and end of the bridge, crawled within, and donned his coat—a ready-made, slop-chest garment, designed for a larger man—and buttoning it around himself and the little girl, lay down on the hard woodwork. She was still crying, but soon, under the influence of the warmth of his body, ceased and went to sleep.

Huddled in a corner, he gave himself up to the torment of his thoughts. Two pictures alternately crowded his mind; one, that of the woman of his dream, entreating him to come back—which his memory clung to as an oracle; the other, of this woman, cold and lifeless, fathoms deep in the sea. He pondered on her chances. She was close to, or on the bridge steps; and boat No. 24, which he was almost sure was being cleared away as he looked, would swing close to her as it descended. She could climb in and be saved—unless the swimmers from doors and hatches should swamp the boat. And, in his agony of mind, he cursed these swimmers, preferring to see her, mentally, the only passenger in the boat, with the watch-on-deck to pull her to safety.

The potent drug he had taken was still at work, and this, with the musical wash of the sea on the icy beach, and the muffled creaking and crackling beneath and around him—the voice of the iceberg—overcame him finally, and he slept, to waken at daylight with limbs stiffened and numb—almost frozen.

And all night, as he slept, a boat with the number twenty-four on her bow, pulled by sturdy sailors and steered by brass-buttoned officers, was making for the Southern Lane—the highway of spring traffic. And, crouched in the stern-sheets of this boat was a moaning, praying woman, who cried and screamed at intervals, for husband and baby, and would not be comforted, even when one of the brass-buttoned officers assured her that her child was safe in the care of John Rowland, a brave and trusty sailor, who was certainly in the other boat with it. He did not tell her, of course, that Rowland had hailed from the berg as she lay unconscious, and that if he still had the child, it was with him there—deserted.

Chapter VIII

Rowland, with some misgivings, drank a small quantity of the liquor, and wrapping the still sleeping child in the coat, stepped out on the ice. The fog was gone and a blue, sailless sea stretched out to the horizon. Behind him was ice—a mountain of it. He climbed the elevation and looked at another stretch of vacant view from a precipice a hundred feet high. To his left the ice sloped to a steeper beach than the one behind him, and to the right, a pile of hummocks and taller peaks, interspersed with numerous cañons and caves, and glistening with waterfalls, shut out the horizon in this direction. Nowhere was there a sail or steamer's smoke to cheer him, and he retraced his steps. When but half-way to the wreckage, he saw a moving white object approaching from the direction of the peaks.

His eyes were not yet in good condition, and after an uncertain scrutiny he started at a run; for he saw that the mysterious white object was nearer the bridge than himself, and rapidly lessening the distance. A hundred yards away, his heart bounded and the blood in his veins felt cold as the ice under foot, for the white object proved to be a traveler from the frozen North, lean and famished—a polar bear, who had scented food and was seeking it—coming on at a lumbering run, with great red jaws half open and yellow fangs exposed. Rowland had no weapon but a strong jackknife, but this he pulled from his pocket and opened as he ran. Not for an instant did he hesitate at a conflict that promised almost certain death; for the presence of this bear involved the safety of a child whose life had become of more importance to him than his own. To his horror, he saw it creep out of the opening in its white covering, just as the bear turned the corner of the bridge.

"Go back, baby, go back," he shouted, as he bounded down the slope. The bear reached the child first, and with seemingly no effort, dashed it, with a blow of its massive paw, a dozen feet away, where it lay quiet. Turning to follow, the brute was met by Rowland.

The bear rose to his haunches, sank down, and charged; and Rowland felt the bones of his left arm crushing under the bite of the big, yellow-fanged jaws. But, falling he buried the knife-blade in the shaggy hide, and the bear, with an angry snarl, spat out the mangled member and dealt him a sweeping blow which sent him farther along the ice than the child had gone. He arose, with broken ribs, and—scarcely feeling the pain—awaited the second charge. Again was the crushed and useless arm gripped in the yellow vise, and again was he pressed backward; but this time he used the knife with method. The great snout was pressing his breast; the hot, fetid breath was in his nostrils; and at his shoulder the hungry eyes were glaring into his own. He struck for the left eye of the brute and struck true. The five-inch blade went in to the handle, piercing the brain, and the animal, with a convulsive spring which carried him half-way to his feet by the wounded arm, reared up, with paws outstretched, to full eight feet of length, then sagged down, and with a few spasmodic kicks, lay still. Rowland had done what no Innuit hunter will attempt—he had fought and killed the Tiger-of-the-North with a knife.

It had all happened in a minute, but in that minute he was crippled for life; for in the quiet of a hospital, the best of surgical skill could hardly avail to reset the fractured particles of bone in the limp arm, and bring to place the crushed ribs. And he was adrift on a floating island of ice, with the temperature near the freezing point, and without even the rude appliances of the savage.

He painfully made his way to the little pile of red and white, and lifted it with his uninjured arm, though the stooping caused him excruciating torture. The child was bleeding from four deep, cruel scratches, extending diagonally from the right shoulder down the back; but he found upon examination that the soft, yielding bones were unbroken, and that her unconsciousness came from the rough contact of the little forehead with the ice; for a large lump had raised.

Of pure necessity, his first efforts must be made in his own behalf; so wrapping the baby in his coat he placed it in his shelter, and cut and made from the canvas a sling for his dangling arm. Then, with knife, fingers, and teeth, he partly skinned the bear—often compelled to pause to save himself from fainting with pain—and cut from the warm but not very thick layer of fat a broad slab, which, after bathing the wounds at a near-by pool, he bound firmly to the little one's back, using the torn night-gown for a bandage.

He cut the flannel lining from his coat, and from that of the sleeves made nether garments for the little limbs, doubling the surplus length over the ankles and tying in place with rope-yarns from a boat-lacing. The body lining he wrapped around her waist, inclosing the arms, and around the whole he passed turn upon turn of canvas in strips, marling the mummy-like bundle with yarns, much as a sailor secures chafing-gear to the doubled parts of a hawser—a process when complete, that would have aroused the indignation of any mother who saw it. But he was only a man, and suffering mental and physical anguish.

By the time he had finished, the child had recovered consciousness, and was protesting its misery in a feeble, wailing cry. But he dared not stop—to become stiffened with cold and pain. There was plenty of fresh water from melting ice, scattered in pools. The bear would furnish food; but they needed fire, to cook this food, keep them warm, and the dangerous inflammation from their hurts, and to raise a smoke to be seen by passing craft.

He recklessly drank from the bottle, needing the stimulant, and reasoning, perhaps rightly, that no ordinary drug could affect him in his present condition; then he examined the wreckage—most of it good kindling wood. Partly above, partly below the pile, was a steel lifeboat, decked over air-tight ends, now doubled to more than a right angle and resting on its side. With canvas hung over one half, and a small fire in the other, it promised, by its conducting property, a warmer and better shelter than the bridge. A sailor without matches is an anomaly. He whittled shavings, kindled the fire, hung the canvas and brought the child, who begged piteously for a drink of water.

He found a tin can—possibly left in a leaky boat before its final hoist to the davits—and gave her a drink, to which he had added a few drops of the whisky. Then he thought of breakfast. Cutting a steak from the hindquarters of the bear, he toasted it on the end of a splinter and found it sweet and satisfying; but when he attempted to feed the child, he understood the necessity of freeing its arms—which he did, sacrificing his left shirtsleeve to cover them. The change and the food stopped its crying for a while, and Rowland lay down with it in the warm boat. Before the day had passed the whisky was gone and he was delirious with fever, while the child was but little better.

Chapter IX

With lucid intervals, during which he replenished or rebuilt the fire, cooked the bear-meat, and fed and dressed the wounds of the child, this delirium lasted three days. His suffering was intense. His arm, the seat of throbbing pain, had swollen to twice the natural size, while his side prevented him taking a full breath, voluntarily. He had paid no attention to his own hurts, and it was either the vigor of a constitution that years of dissipation had not impaired, or some anti-febrile property of bear-meat, or the absence of the exciting whisky that won the battle. He rekindled the fire with his last match on the evening of the third day and looked around the darkening horizon, sane, but feeble in body and mind.

If a sail had appeared in the interim, he had not seen it; nor was there one in sight now. Too weak to climb the slope, he returned to the boat, where the child, exhausted from fruitless crying, was now sleeping. His unskillful and rather heroic manner of wrapping it up to protect it from cold had, no doubt, contributed largely to the closing of its wounds by forcibly keeping it still, though it must have added to its present sufferings. He looked for a moment on the wan, tear-stained little face, with its fringe of tangled curls peeping above the wrappings of canvas, and stooping painfully down, kissed it softly; but the kiss awakened it and it cried for its mother. He could not soothe it, nor could he try; and with a formless, wordless curse against destiny welling up from his heart, he left it and sat down on the wreckage at some distance away.

"We'll very likely get well," he mused, gloomily, "unless I let the fire go out. What then? We can't last longer than the berg, and not much longer than the bear. We must be out of the tracks—we were about nine hundred miles out when we struck; and the current sticks to the fog-belt here—about west-sou'west—but that's the surface water. These deep fellows have currents of their own. There's no fog; we must be to the southward of the belt—between the Lanes. They'll run their boats in the other Lane after this. I think—the money-grabbing wretches. Curse them—if they've drowned her. Curse them, with their water-tight compartments, and their logging of the lookouts. Twenty-four boats for three thousand people—lashed down with tarred gripe-lashings—thirty men to clear them away, and not an axe on the boat-deck or a sheath-knife on a man. Could she have got away? If they got that boat down, they might have taken her in from the steps; and the mate knew I had her child—he would tell her. Her name must be Myra, too; it was her voice I heard in that dream. That was hasheesh. What did they drug me for? But the whisky was all right. It's all done with now, unless I get ashore—but will I?

The moon rose above the castellated structure to the left, flooding the icy beach with ashen-gray light, sparkling in a thousand points from the cascades, streams, and rippling pools, throwing into blackest shadow the gullies and hollows, and bringing to his mind, in spite of the weird beauty of the scene, a crushing sense of loneliness—of littleness—as though the vast pile of inorganic desolation which held him was of far greater importance than himself, and all the hopes, plans, and fears of his lifetime. The child had cried itself to sleep again, and he paced up and down the ice.

"Up there," he said, moodily, looking into the sky, where a few stars shone faintly in the flood from the moon; "Up there—somewhere—they don't know just where—but somewhere up above, is the Christians' Heaven. Up there is their good God—who has placed Myra's child here—their good God whom they borrowed from the savage, bloodthirsty race that invented him. And down below us—somewhere again—is their hell and their bad god, whom they invented themselves. And they give us our choice—Heaven or hell. It is not so—not so. The great mystery is not solved—the human heart is not helped in this way. No good, merciful God created this world or its conditions. Whatever may be the nature of the causes at work beyond our mental vision, one fact is indubitably proven—that the qualities of mercy, goodness, justice, play no part in the governing scheme. And yet, they say the core of all religions on earth is the belief in this. Is it? Or is it the cowardly, human fear of the unknown—that impels the savage mother to throw her babe to a crocodile—that impels the civilized man to endow churches—that has kept in existence from the beginning a class of soothsayers, medicine-men, priests, and clergymen, all living on the hopes and fears excited by themselves.

"And people pray—millions of them—and claim they are answered. Are they? Was ever supplication sent into that sky by troubled humanity answered, or even heard? Who knows? They pray for rain and sunshine, and both come in time. They pray for health and success and both are but natural in the marching of events. This is not evidence. But they say that they know, by spiritual uplifting, that they are heard, and comforted, and answered at the moment. Is not this a physiological experiment? Would they not feel equally tranquil if they repeated the multiplication table, or boxed the compass?

"Millions have believed this—that prayers are answered—and these millions have prayed to different gods. Were they all wrong or all right? Would a tentative prayer be listened to? Admitting that the Bibles, and Korans, and Vedas, are misleading and unreliable, may there not be an unseen, unknown Being, who knows my heart—who is watching me now? If so, this Being gave me my reason, which doubts Him, and on Him is the responsibility. And would this being, if he exists, overlook a defect for which I am not to blame, and listen to a prayer from me, based on the mere chance that I might be mistaken? Can an unbeliever, in the full strength of his reasoning powers, come to such trouble that he can no longer stand alone, but must cry for help to an imagined power? Can such time come to a sane man—to me?" He looked at the dark line of vacant horizon. It was seven miles away; New York was nine hundred; the moon in the east over two hundred thousand, and the stars above, any number of billions. He was alone, with a sleeping child, a dead bear, and the Unknown. He walked softly to the boat and looked at the little one for a moment; then, raising his head, he whispered: "For you, Myra."

Sinking to his knees the atheist lifted his eyes to the heavens, and with his feeble voice and the fervor born of helplessness, prayed to the God that he denied. He begged for the life of the waif in his care—for the safety of the mother, so needful to the little one—and for courage and strength to do his part and bring them together. But beyond the appeal for help in the service of others, not one word or expressed thought of his prayer included himself as a beneficiary. So much for pride. As he rose to his feet, the flying-jib of a bark appeared around the corner of ice to the right of the beach, and a moment later the whole moon-lit fabric came into view, wafted along by the faint westerly air, not half a mile away.

He sprang to the fire, forgetting his pain, and throwing on wood, made a blaze. He hailed, in a frenzy of excitement: "Bark ahoy! Bark ahoy! Take us off," and a deep-toned answer came across the water.

"Wake up, Myra," he cried, as he lifted the child; "wake up. We're going away."

"We're goin' to mamma?" she asked, with no symptoms of crying.

"Yes, we're going to mamma, now—that is," he added to himself; "if that clause in the prayer is considered."

Fifteen minutes later as he watched the approach of a white quarter-boat, he muttered: "That bark was there—half a mile back in this wind—before I thought of praying. Is that prayer answered? Is she safe?"

Chapter X

On the first floor of the London Royal Exchange is a large apartment studded with desks, around and between which surges a hurrying, shouting crowd of brokers, clerks, and messengers. Fringing this apartment are doors and hallways leading to adjacent rooms and offices, and scattered through it are bulletin-boards, on which are daily written in duplicate the marine casualties of the world. At one end is a raised platform, sacred to the presence of an important functionary. In the technical language of the "City," the apartment is known as the "Room," and the functionary, as the "Caller," whose business it is to call out in a mighty sing-song voice the names of members wanted at the door, and the bare particulars of bulletin news prior to its being chalked out for reading.

It is the headquarters of Lloyds—the immense association of underwriters, brokers, and shipping-men, which, beginning with the customers at Edward Lloyd's coffee-house in the latter part of the seventeenth century, has, retaining his name for a title, developed into a corporation so well equipped, so splendidly organized and powerful, that kings and ministers of state appeal to it at times for foreign news.

Not a master or mate sails under the English flag but whose record, even to forecastle fights, is tabulated at Lloyds for the inspection of prospective employers. Not a ship is cast away on any inhabitable coast of the world, during underwriters' business hours, but what that mighty sing-songery announces the event at Lloyds within thirty minutes.

One of the adjoining rooms is known as the Chartroom. Here can be found in perfect order and sequence, each on its roller, the newest charts of all nations, with a library of nautical literature describing to the last detail the harbors, lights, rocks, shoals, and sailing directions of every coast-line shown on the charts; the tracks of latest storms; the changes of ocean currents, and the whereabouts of derelicts and icebergs. A member at Lloyds acquires in time a theoretical knowledge of the sea seldom exceeded by the men who navigate it.

Another apartment—the Captain's room—is given over to joy and refreshment, and still another, the antithesis of the last, is the Intelligence office, where anxious ones inquire for and are told the latest news of this or that overdue ship.

On the day when the assembled throng of underwriters and brokers had been thrown into an uproarious panic the Crier's announcement that the great *Titan* was destroyed, and the papers of Europe and America were issuing extras giving the meager details of the arrival at New York of one boat-load of her people, this office had been crowded with weeping women and worrying men, who would ask, and remain to ask again, for more news. And when it came—a later cablegram,—giving the story of the wreck and the names of the captain, first officer, boatswain, seven sailors, and one lady passenger as those of the saved, a feeble old gentleman had raised his voice in a quavering scream, high above the sobbing of women, and said:

"My daughter-in-law is safe; but where is my son,—where is my son, and my grandchild?" Then he had hurried away, but was back again the next day, and the next. And when, on the tenth day of waiting and watching, he learned of another boat-load of sailors and children arrived at Gibraltar, he shook his head, slowly, muttering: "George, George," and left the room. That night, after telegraphing the consul at Gibraltar of his coming, he crossed the channel.

In the first tumultuous riot of inquiry, when underwriters had climbed over desks and each other to hear again of the wreck of the *Titan,* one—the noisiest of all, a corpulent, hook-nosed man with flashing black eyes—had broken away from the crowd and made his way to the Captain's room, where, after a draught of brandy, he had seated himself heavily, with a groan that came from his soul.

"Father Abraham," he muttered; "this will ruin me."

Others came in, some to drink, some to condole—all, to talk.

"Hard hit, Meyer?" asked one.

"Ten thousand," he answered, gloomily.

"Serve you right," said another, unkindly; "have more baskets for your eggs. Knew you'd bring up."

Though Mr. Meyer's eyes sparkled at this, he said nothing, but drank himself stupid and was assisted home by one of his clerks. From this on, neglecting his business—excepting to occasionally visit the bulletins—he spent his time in the Captain's room drinking heavily, and bemoaning his luck. On the tenth day he read with watery eyes, posted on the bulletin below the news of the arrival at Gibraltar of the second boat-load of people, the following:

"Life-buoy of *Royal Age,* London, picked up among wreckage
in Lat. 45-20, N. Lon. 54-31 W. Ship *Arctic,* Boston, Capt. Brandt."

"Oh, mine good God," he howled, as he rushed toward the Captain's room.

"Poor devil—poor damn fool of an Israelite," said one observer to another. "He covered the whole of the *Royal Age,* and the biggest chunk of the *Titan.* It'll take his wife's diamonds to settle."

Three weeks later, Mr. Meyer was aroused from a brooding lethargy, by a crowd of shouting underwriters, who rushed into the Captain's room, seized him by the shoulders, and hurried him out and up to a bulletin.

"Read it, Meyer—read it. What d'you think of it?" With some difficulty he read aloud, while they watched his face:

"John Rowland, sailor of the *Titan,* with child passenger, name
unknown, on board *Peerless,* Bath, at Christiansand, Norway. Both
dangerously ill. Rowland speaks of ship cut in half night before loss
of *Titan.*"

"What do you make of it, Meyer—*Royal Age,* isn't it?" asked one.

"Yes," vociferated another, "I've figured back. Only ship not reported lately. Overdue two months. Was spoken same day fifty miles east of that iceberg."

"Sure thing," said others. "Nothing said about it in the captain's statement—looks queer."

"Vell, vwhat of it," said Mr. Meyer, painfully and stupidly: "dere is a collision clause in der *Titan's* policy; I merely bay the money to der steamship company instead of to der *Royal Age* beeple."

"But why did the captain conceal it?" they shouted at him. "What's his object—assured against collision suits."

"Der looks of it, berhaps—looks pad."

"Nonsense, Meyer, what's the matter with you? Which one of the lost tribes did you spring from—you're like none of your race—drinking yourself stupid like a good Christian. I've got a thousand on the *Titan,* and if I'm to pay it I want to know why. You've got the heaviest risk and the brain to fight for it—you've got to do it. Go home, straighten up, and attend to this. We'll watch Rowland till you take hold. We're all caught."

They put him into a cab, took him to a Turkish bath, and then home.

The next morning he was at his desk, clear-eyed and clear-headed, and for a few weeks was a busy, scheming man of business.

Chapter XI

On a certain morning, about two months after the announcement of the loss of the *Titan,* Mr. Meyer sat at his desk in the Rooms, busily writing, when the old gentleman who had bewailed the death of his son in the Intelligence office tottered in and took a chair beside him.

"Good morning, Mr. Selfridge," he said, scarcely looking up; "I suppose you have come to see der insurance paid over. Der sixty days are up."

"Yes, yes, Mr. Meyer," said the old gentleman, wearily; "of course, as merely a stockholder, I can take no active part; but I am a member here, and naturally a little anxious. All I had in the world—even to my son and grandchild—was in the *Titan."*

"It is very sad, Mr. Selfridge; you have my deepest sympathy. I pelieve you are der largest holder of *Titan* stock—about one hundred thousand, is it not?"

"About that."

"I am der heaviest insurer; so Mr. Selfridge, this battle will be largely petween you and myself."

"Battle—is there to be any difficulty?" asked Mr. Selfridge, anxiously.

"Berhaps—I do not know. Der underwriters and outside companies have blaced matters in my hands and will not bay until I take der initiative. We must hear from one John Rowland, who, with a little child, was rescued from der berg and taken to Christiansand. He has been too sick to leave der ship which found him and is coming up der Thames in her this morning. I have a carriage at der dock and expect him at my office py noon. Dere is where we will dransact this little pizness—not here."

"A child—saved," queried the old gentleman; "dear me, it may be little Myra. She was not at Gibraltar with the others. I would not care—I would not care much about the money, if she was safe. But my son—my only son—is gone; and, Mr. Meyer, I am a ruined man if this insurance is not paid."

"And I am a ruined man if it is," said Mr. Meyer, rising. "Will you come around to der office, Mr. Selfridge? I expect der attorney and Captain Bryce are dere now." Mr. Selfridge arose and accompanied him to the street.

A rather meagerly-furnished private office in Threadneedle Street, partitioned off from a larger one bearing Mr. Meyer's name in the window, received the two men, one of whom, in the interests of good business, was soon to be impoverished. They had not waited a minute before Captain Bryce and Mr. Austen were announced and ushered in. Sleek, well-fed, and gentlemanly in manner, perfect types of the British naval officer, they bowed politely to Mr. Selfridge when Mr. Meyer introduced them as the captain and first officer of the *Titan,* and seated themselves. A few moments later brought a shrewd-looking person whom Mr. Meyer addressed as the attorney for the steamship company, but did not introduce; for such are the amenities of the English system of caste.

"Now then, gentlemen," said Mr. Meyer, "I pelieve we can proceed to pizness up to a certain point—berhaps further. Mr. Thompson, you have the affidavit of Captain Bryce?"

"I have," said the attorney, producing a document which Mr. Meyer glanced at and handed back.

"And in this statement, captain," he said, "you have sworn that der voyage was uneventful up to der moment of der wreck—that is," he added, with an oily smile, as he noticed the paling of the captain's face—"that nothing occurred to make der *Titan* less seaworthy or manageable?"

"That is what I swore to," said the captain, with a little sigh.

"You are part owner, are you not, Captain Bryce?"

"I own five shares of the company's stock."

"I have examined der charter and der company lists," said Mr. Meyer; "each boat of der company is, so far as assessments and dividends are concerned, a separate company. I find you are listed as owning two sixty-seconds of der *Titan* stock. This makes you, under der law, part owner of der *Titan,* and responsible as such."

"What do you mean, sir, by that word responsible?" said Captain Bryce, quickly.

For answer, Mr. Meyer elevated his black eyebrows, assumed an attitude of listening, looked at his watch and went to the door, which, as he opened, admitted the sound of carriage wheels.

"In here," he called to his clerks, then faced the captain.

"What do I mean, Captain Bryce?" he thundered. "I mean that you have concealed in your sworn statement all reference to der fact that you collided with and sunk the ship *Royal Age* on der night before the wreck of your own ship."

"Who says so—how do you know it?" blustered the captain. "You have only that bulletin statement of the man Rowland—an irresponsible drunkard."

"The man was lifted aboard drunk at New York," broke in the first officer, "and remained in a condition of delirium tremens up to the shipwreck. We did not meet the *Royal Age* and are in no way responsible for her loss."

"Yes," added Captain Bryce, "and a man in that condition is liable to see anything. We listened to his ravings on the night of the wreck. He was on lookout—on the bridge. Mr. Austen, the boats'n, and myself were close to him."

Before Mr. Meyer's oily smile had indicated to the flustered captain that he had said too much, the door opened and admitted Rowland, pale, and weak, with empty left sleeve, leaning on the arm of a bronze-bearded and manly-looking giant who carried little Myra on the other shoulder, and who said, in the breezy tone of the quarter-deck:

"Well, I've brought him, half dead; but why couldn't you give me time to dock my ship? A mate can't do everything."

"And this is Captain Barry, of der *Peerless,*" said Mr. Meyer, taking his hand. "It is all right, my friend; you will not lose. And this is Mr. Rowland—and this is der little child. Sit down, my friend. I congratulate you on your escape."

"Thank you," said Rowland, weakly, as he seated himself; "they cut my arm off at Christiansand, and I still live. That is my escape."

Captain Bryce and Mr. Austen, pale and motionless, stared hard at this man, in whose emaciated face, refined by suffering to the almost spiritual softness of age, they hardly recognized the features of the troublesome sailor of the *Titan*. His clothing, though clean, was ragged and patched.

Mr. Selfridge had arisen and was also staring, not at Rowland, but at the child, who, seated in the lap of the big Captain Barry, was looking around with wondering eyes. Her costume was unique. A dress of bagging-stuff, put together—as were her canvas shoes and hat—with sail-twine in sail-makers' stitches, three to the inch, covered skirts and underclothing made from old flannel shirts. It represented many an hour's work of the watch-below, lovingly bestowed by the crew of the *Peerless;* for the crippled Rowland could not sew. Mr. Selfridge approached, scanned the pretty features closely; and asked:

"What is her name?"

"Her first name is Myra," answered Rowland. "She remembers that; but I have not learned her last name, though I knew her mother years ago—before her marriage."

"Myra, Myra," repeated the old gentleman; "do you know me? Don't you know me?" He trembled visibly as he stooped and kissed her. The little forehead puckered and wrinkled as the child struggled with memory; then it cleared and the whole face sweetened to a smile.

"Gwampa," she said.

"Oh, God, I thank thee," murmured Mr. Selfridge, taking her in his arms. "I have lost my son, but I have found his child—my granddaughter."

"But, sir," asked Rowland, eagerly; "you—this child's grandfather? Your son is lost, you say? Was he on board the *Titan?* And the mother—was she saved, or is she, too—" he stopped unable to continue.

"The mother is safe—in New York; but the father, my son, has not yet been heard from," said the old man, mournfully.

Rowland's head sank and he hid his face for a moment in his arm, on the table at which he sat. It had been a face as old, and worn, and weary as that of the white-haired man confronting him. On it, when it raised—flushed, bright-eyed and smiling—was the glory of youth.

"I trust, sir," he said, "that you will telegraph her. I am penniless at present, and, besides, do not know her name."

"Selfridge—which, of course, is my own name. Mrs. Colonel, or Mrs. George Selfridge. Our New York address is well known. But I shall cable her at once; and, believe me, sir, although I can understand that our debt to you cannot be named in terms of money, you need not be penniless long. You are evidently a capable man, and I have wealth and influence."

Rowland merely bowed, slightly, but Mr. Meyer muttered to himself: "Vealth and influence. Berhaps not. Now, gentlemen," he added, in a louder tone, "to pizness. Mr. Rowland, will you tell us about der running down of der *Royal Age?*"

"Was it the *Royal Age?*" asked Rowland. "I sailed in her one voyage. Yes, certainly."

Mr. Selfridge, more interested in Myra than in the coming account, carried her over to a chair in the corner and sat down, where he fondled and talked to her after the manner of grandfathers the world over, and Rowland, first looking steadily into the faces of the two men he had come to expose, and whose presence he had thus far ignored, told, while they held their teeth tight together and often buried their finger-nails in their palms, the terrible story of the cutting in half of the ship on the first night out from New York, finishing with the attempted bribery and his refusal.

"Vell, gentlemen, vwhat do you think of that?" asked Mr. Meyer, looking around.

"A lie, from beginning to end," stormed Captain Bryce.

Rowland rose to his feet, but was pressed back by the big man who had accompanied him—who then faced Captain Bryce and said quietly:

"I saw a polar bear that this man killed in open fight. I saw his arm afterward, and while nursing him away from death I heard no whines or complaints. He can fight his own battles when well, and when sick I'll do it for him. If you insult him again in my presence I'll knock your teeth down your throat."

Chapter XII

There was a moment's silence while the two captains eyed one another, broken by the attorney, who said:

"Whether this story is true or false, it certainly has no bearing on the validity of the policy. If this happened, it was after the policy attached and before the wreck of the *Titan.*"

"But der concealment," shouted Mr. Meyer, excitedly.

"Has no bearing, either. If he concealed anything it was done after the wreck, and after your liability was confirmed. It was not even barratry. You must pay this insurance."

"I will not bay it. I will not. I will fight you in der courts." Mr. Meyer stamped up and down the floor in his excitement, then stopped with a triumphant smile, and shook his finger into the face of the attorney.

"And even if der concealment will not vitiate der policy, der fact that he had a drunken man on lookout when der *Titan* struck der iceberg will be enough. Go ahead and sue. I will not pay. He was part owner."

"You have no witnesses to that admission," said the attorney. Mr. Meyer looked around the group and the smile left his face.

"Captain Bryce was mistaken," said Mr. Austen. "This man was drunk at New York, like others of the crew. But he was sober and competent when on lookout. I discussed theories of navigation with him during his trick on the bridge that night and he spoke intelligently."

"But you yourself said, not ten minutes ago, that this man was in a state of delirium tremens up to der collision," said Mr. Meyer.

"What I said and what I will admit under oath are two different things," said the officer, desperately. "I may have said anything under the excitement of the moment—when we were accused of such an infamous crime. I say now, that John Rowland, whatever may have been his condition on the preceding night, was a sober and competent lookout at the time of the wreck of the *Titan.*"

"Thank you," said Rowland, dryly, to the first officer; then, looking into the appealing face of Mr. Meyer, he said:

"I do not think it will be necessary to brand me before the world as an inebriate in order to punish the company and these men. Barratry, as I understand it, is the unlawful act of a captain or crew at sea, causing damage or loss; and it only applies when the parties are purely employees. Did I understand rightly—that Captain Bryce was part owner of the *Titan?*"

"Yes," said Mr. Meyer, "he owns stock; and we insure against barratry; but this man, as part owner, could not fall back on it."

"And an unlawful act," went on Rowland, "perpetrated by a captain who is part owner, which might cause shipwreck, and, during the perpetration of which shipwreck, really occurs, will be sufficient to void the policy."

"Certainly," said Mr. Meyer, eagerly. "You were drunk on der lookout—you were raving drunk, as he said himself. You will swear to this, will you not, my friend? It is bad faith with der underwriters. It annuls der insurance. You admit this, Mr. Thompson, do you not?"

"That is law," said the attorney, coldly.

"Was Mr. Austen a part owner, also?" asked Rowland, ignoring Mr. Meyer's view of the case.

"One share, is it not, Mr. Austen?" asked Mr. Meyer, while he rubbed his hands and smiled. Mr. Austen made no sign of denial and Rowland continued:

"Then, for drugging a sailor into a stupor, and having him on lookout out of his turn while in that condition, and at the moment when the *Titan* struck the iceberg, Captain Bryce and Mr. Austen have, as part owners, committed an act which nullifies the insurance on that ship."

"You infernal, lying scoundrel!" roared Captain Bryce. He strode toward Rowland with threatening face. Half-way, he was stopped by the impact of a huge brown fist which sent him reeling and staggering across the room toward Mr. Selfridge and the child, over whom he floundered to the floor—a disheveled heap,—while the big Captain Barry examined teeth-marks on his knuckles, and every one else sprang to their feet.

"I told you to look out," said Captain Barry. "Treat my friend respectfully." He glared steadily at the first officer, as though inviting him to duplicate the offense; but that gentleman backed away from him and assisted the dazed Captain Bryce to a chair, where he felt of his loosened teeth, spat blood upon Mr. Meyer's floor, and gradually awakened to a realization of the fact that he had been knocked down—and by an American.

Little Myra, unhurt but badly frightened, began to cry and call for Rowland in her own way, to the wonder, and somewhat to the scandal of the gentle old man who was endeavoring to soothe her.

"Dammy," she cried, as she struggled to go to him; "I want Dammy—Dammy—Da-a-may."

"Oh, what a pad little girl," said the jocular Mr. Meyer, looking down on her. "Where did you learn such language?"

"It is my nickname," said Rowland, smiling in spite of himself. "She has coined the word," he explained to the agitated Mr. Selfridge, who had not yet comprehended what had happened; "and I have not yet been able to persuade her to drop it—and I could not be harsh with her. Let me take her, sir." He seated himself, with the child, who nestled up to him contentedly and soon was tranquil.

"Now, my friend," said Mr. Meyer, "you must tell us about this drugging." Then while Captain Bryce, under the memory of the blow he had received, nursed himself into an insane fury; and Mr. Austen, with his hand resting lightly on the captain's shoulder ready to restrain him, listened to the story; and the attorney drew up a chair and took notes of the story; and Mr. Selfridge drew his chair close to Myra and paid no attention to the story at all, Rowland recited the events prior to and succeeding the shipwreck. Beginning with the finding of the whisky in his pocket he told of his being called to the starboard bridge lookout in place of the rightful incumbent; of the sudden and strange interest Mr. Austen displayed as to his knowledge of navigation; of the pain in his stomach, the frightful shapes he had seen on the deck beneath and the sensations of his dream—leaving out only the part which bore on the woman he loved; he told of the sleep-walking child which awakened him, of the crash of ice and instant wreck, and the fixed condition of his eyes which prevented their focusing only at a certain distance, finishing his story—to explain his empty sleeve—with a graphic account of the fight with the bear.

"And I have studied it all out," he said, in conclusion. "I was drugged—I believe, with hasheesh, which makes a man see strange things—and brought up on the bridge lookout where I could be watched and my ravings listened to and recorded, for the sole purpose of discrediting my threatened testimony in regard to the collision of the night before. But I was only half-drugged, as I spilled part of my tea at supper. In that tea, I am positive, was the hasheesh."

"You know all about it, don't you," snarled Captain Bryce, from his chair, "'twas not hasheesh; 'twas an infusion of Indian hemp; you don't know—" Mr. Austen's hand closed over his mouth and he subsided.

"Self-convicted," said Rowland, with a quiet laugh. "Hasheesh is made from Indian hemp."

"You hear this, gentlemen," exclaimed Mr. Meyer, springing to his feet and facing everybody in turn. He pounced on Captain Barry. "You hear this confession, captain; you hear him say Indian hemp? I have a witness now, Mr. Thompson. Go right on with your suit. You hear him, Captain Barry. You are disinterested. You are a witness. You hear?"

"Yes, I heard it—the murdering scoundrel," said the captain.

Mr. Meyer danced up and down in his joy, while the attorney, pocketing his notes, remarked to the discomfited Captain Bryce: "You are the poorest fool I know," and left the office.

Then Mr. Meyer calmed himself, and facing the two steamship officers, said, slowly and impressively, while he poked his forefinger almost into their faces:

"England is a fine country, my friends—a fine country to leave pehind sometimes. Dere is Canada, and der United States, and Australia, and South Africa—all fine countries, too—fine countries to go to with new names. My friends, you will be bulletened and listed at Lloyds in less than half an hour, and you will never again sail under der English flag as officers. And, my friends, let me say, that in half an hour after you are bulletened, all Scotland Yard will be looking for you. But my door is not locked."

Silently they arose, pale, shamefaced, and crushed, and went out the door, through the outer office, and into the street.

Chapter XIII

Mr. Selfridge had begun to take an interest in the proceedings. As the two men passed out he arose and asked:

"Have you reached a settlement, Mr. Meyer? Will the insurance be paid?"

"No," roared the underwriter, in the ear of the puzzled old gentleman; while he slapped him vigorously on the back; "it will not be paid. You or I must have been ruined, Mr. Selfridge, and it has settled on you. I do not pay der *Titan's* insurance—nor will der other insurers. On der contrary, as der collision clause in der policy is void with der rest, your company must reimburse me for der insurance which I must pay to der *Royal Age* owners—that is, unless our good friend here, Mr. Rowland, who was on der lookout at der time, will swear that her lights were out."

"Not at all," said Rowland. "Her lights were burning—look to the old gentleman," he exclaimed. "Look out for him. Catch him!"

Mr. Selfridge was stumbling toward a chair. He grasped it, loosened his hold, and before anyone could reach him, fell to the floor, where he lay, with ashen lips and rolling eyes, gasping convulsively.

"Heart failure," said Rowland, as he knelt by his side. "Send for a doctor."

"Send for a doctor," repeated Mr. Meyer through the door to his clerks; "and send for a carriage, quick. I don't want him to die in der office."

Captain Barry lifted the helpless figure to a couch, and they watched, while the convulsions grew easier, the breath shorter, and the lips from ashen gray to blue. Before a doctor or carriage had come, he had passed away.

"Sudden emotion of some kind," said the doctor when he did arrive. "Violent emotion, too. Hear bad news?"

"Bad and good," answered the underwriter. "Good, in learning that this dear little girl was his granddaughter—bad, in learning that he was a ruined man. He was der heaviest stockholder in der *Titan.* One hundred thousand pounds, he owned, of der stock, all of which this poor, dear little child will not get." Mr. Meyer looked sorrowful, as he patted Myra on the head.

Captain Barry beckoned to Rowland, who, slightly flushed, was standing by the still figure on the couch and watching the face of Mr. Meyer, on which annoyance, jubilation, and simulated shock could be seen in turn.

"Wait," he said, as he turned to watch the doctor leave the room. "Is this so, Mr. Meyer," he added to the underwriter, "that Mr. Selfridge owned *Titan* stock, and would have been ruined, had he lived, by the loss of the insurance money?"

"Yes, he would have been a poor man. He had invested his last farthing—one hundred thousand pounds. And if he had left any more it would be assessed to make good his share of what der company must bay for der *Royal Age,* which I also insured."

"Was there a collision clause in the *Titan's* policy?"

"Dere was."

"And you took the risk, knowing that she was to run the Northern Lane at full speed through fog and snow?"

"I did—so did others."

"Then, Mr. Meyer, it remains for me to tell you that the insurance on the *Titan* will be paid, as well as any liabilities included in and specified by the collision clause in the policy. In short, I, the one man who can prevent it, refuse to testify."

"Vwhat-a-t?"

Mr. Meyer grasped the back of a chair and, leaning over it, stared at Rowland.

"You will not testify? Vwhat you mean?"

"What I said; and I do not feel called upon to give you my reasons, Mr. Meyer."

"My good friend," said the underwriter, advancing with out-stretched hands to Rowland, who backed away, and taking Myra by the hand, moved toward the door. Mr. Meyer sprang ahead, locked it and removed the key, and faced them.

"Oh, mine goot Gott," he shouted, relapsing in his excitement into the more pronounced dialect of his race; "vwhat I do to you, hey? Vwhy you go pack on me, hey? Haf I not bay der doctor's bill? Haf I not bay for der carriage? Haf I not treat you like one shentleman? Haf I not, hey? I sit you down in mine office and call you Mr. Rowland. Haf I not been one shentleman?"

"Open that door," said Rowland, quietly.

"Yes, open it," repeated Captain Barry, his puzzled face clearing at the prospect of action on his part. "Open it or I'll kick it down."

"But you, mine friend—heard der admission of der captain—of der drugging. One goot witness will do: two is petter. But you will swear, mine friend, you will not ruin me."

"I stand by Rowland," said the captain, grimly. "I don't remember what was said, anyhow; got a blamed bad memory. Get away from that door."

Grievous lamentation—weepings and wailings, and the most genuine gnashing of teeth—interspersed with the feebler cries of the frightened Myra and punctuated by terse commands in regard to the door, filled that private office, to the wonder of the clerks without, and ended, at last, with the crashing of the door from its hinges.

Captain Barry, Rowland, and Myra, followed by a parting, heart-borne malediction from the agitated underwriter, left the office and reached the street. The carriage that had brought them was still waiting.

"Settle inside," called the captain to the driver. "We'll take another, Rowland."

Around the first corner they found a cab, which they entered, Captain Barry giving the driver the direction—"Bark *Peerless,* East India Dock."

"I think I understand the game, Rowland," he said, as they started; "you don't want to break this child."

"That's it," answered Rowland, weakly, as he leaned back on the cushion, faint from the excitement of the last few moments. "And as for the right or wrong of the position I am in—why, we must go farther back for it than the question of lookouts. The cause of the wreck was full speed in a fog. All hands on lookout could not have seen that berg. The underwriters knew the speed and took the risk. Let them pay."

"Right—and I'm with you on it. But you must get out of the country. I don't know the law on the matter, but they may compel you to testify. You can't ship 'fore the mast again—that's settled. But you can have a berth mate with me as long as I sail a ship—if you'll take it; and you're to make my cabin your home as long as you like; remember that. Still, I know you want to get across with the kid, and if you stay around until I sail it may be months before you get to New York, with the chance of losing her by getting foul of English law. But just leave it to me. There are powerful interests at stake in regard to this matter."

What Captain Barry had in mind, Rowland was too weak to inquire. On their arrival at the bark he was assisted by his friend to a couch in the cabin, where he spent the rest of the day, unable to leave it. Meanwhile, Captain Barry had gone ashore again.

Returning toward evening, he said to the man on the couch: "I've got your pay, Rowland, and signed a receipt for it to that attorney. He paid it out of his own pocket. You could have worked that company for fifty thousand, or more; but I knew you wouldn't touch their money, and so, only struck him for your wages. You're entitled to a month's pay. Here it is—American money—about seventeen." He gave Rowland a roll of bills.

"Now here's something else, Rowland," he continued, producing an envelope. "In consideration of the fact that you lost all your clothes and later, your arm, through the carelessness of the company's officers, Mr. Thompson offers you this." Rowland opened the envelope. In it were two first cabin tickets from Liverpool to New York. Flushing hotly, he said, bitterly:

"It seems that I'm not to escape it, after all."

"Take 'em, old man, take 'em; in fact, I took 'em for you, and you and the kid are booked. And I made Thompson agree to settle your doctor's bill and expenses with that Sheeny. 'Tisn't bribery. I'd heel you myself for the run over, but, hang it, you'll take nothing from me. You've got to get the young un over. You're the only one to do it. The old gentleman was an American, alone here—hadn't even a lawyer, that I could find. The boat sails in the morning and the night train leaves in two hours. Think of that mother, Rowland. Why, man, I'd travel round the world to stand in your shoes when you hand Myra over. I've got a child of my own." The captain's eyes were winking hard and fast, and Rowland's were shining.

"Yes, I'll take the passage," he said, with a smile. "I accept the bribe."

"That's right. You'll be strong and healthy when you land, and when that mother's through thanking you, and you have to think of yourself, remember—I want a mate and will be here a month before sailing. Write to me, care o' Lloyds, if you want the berth, and I'll send you advance money to get back with."

"Thank you, captain," said Rowland, as he took the other's hand and then glanced at his empty sleeve; "but my going to sea is ended. Even a mate needs two hands."

"Well, suit yourself, Rowland; I'll take you mate without any hands at all while you had your brains. It's done me good to meet a man like you; and—say, old man, you won't take it wrong from me, will you? It's none o' my business, but you're too all-fired good a man to drink. You haven't had a nip for two months. Are you going to begin?"

"Never again," said Rowland, rising. "I've a future now, as well as a past."

Chapter XIV

It was near noon of the next day that Rowland, seated in a steamer-chair with Myra and looking out on a sail-spangled stretch of blue from the saloon-deck of a west-bound liner, remembered that he had made no provisions to have Mrs. Selfridge notified by cable of the safety of her child; and unless Mr. Meyer or his associates gave the story to the press it would not be known.

"Well," he mused, "joy will not kill, and I shall witness it in its fullness if I take her by surprise. But the chances are that it will get into the papers before I reach her. It is too good for Mr. Meyer to keep."

But the story was not given out immediately. Mr. Meyer called a conference of the underwriters concerned with him in the insurance of the *Titan* at which it was decided to remain silent concerning the card they hoped to play, and to spend a little time and money in hunting for other witnesses among the *Titan's* crew, and in interviewing Captain Barry, to the end of improving his memory. A few stormy meetings with this huge obstructionist convinced them of the futility of further effort in his direction, and, after finding at the end of a week that every surviving member of the *Titan's* port watch, as well as a few of the other, had been induced to sign for Cape voyages, or had otherwise disappeared, they decided to give the story told by Rowland to the press in the hope that publicity would avail to bring to light cor-roboratory evidence.

And this story, improved upon in the repeating by Mr. Meyer to reporters, and embellished still further by the reporters as they wrote it up, particularly in the part pertaining to the polar bear,—blazoned out in the great dailies of England and the Continent, and was cabled to New York, with the name of the steamer in which John Rowland had sailed (for his movements had been traced in the search for evidence), where it arrived, too late for publication, the morning of the day on which, with Myra on his shoulder, he stepped down the gangplank at a North River dock. As a consequence, he was surrounded on the dock by enthusiastic reporters, who spoke of the story and asked for details. He refused to talk, escaped them, and gaining the side streets, soon found himself in crowded Broadway, where he entered the office of the steamship company in whose employ he had been wrecked, and secured from the *Titan's* passenger-list the address of Mrs. Selfridge—the only woman saved. Then he took a car up Broadway and alighted abreast of a large department store.

"We're going to see mamma, soon, Myra," he whispered in the pink ear; "and you must go dressed up. It don't matter about me; but you're a Fifth Avenue baby—a little aristocrat. These old clothes won't do, now." But she had forgotten the word "mamma," and was more interested in the exciting noise and life of the street than in the clothing she wore. In the store, Rowland asked for, and was directed to the children's department, where a young woman waited on him.

"This child has been shipwrecked," he said. "I have sixteen dollars and a half to spend on it. Give it a bath, dress its hair, and use up the money on a dress, shoes, and stockings, underclothing, and a hat." The young woman stooped and kissed the little girl from sheer sympathy, but protested that not much could be done.

"Do your best," said Rowland; "it is all I have. I will wait here."

An hour later, penniless again, he emerged from the store with Myra, bravely dressed in her new finery, and was stopped at the corner by a policeman who had seen him come out, and who marveled doubtless, at such juxtaposition of rags and ribbons.

"Whose kid ye got?" he demanded.

"I believe it is the daughter of Mrs. Colonel Selfridge," answered Rowland, haughtily—too haughtily, by far.

"Ye believe—but ye don't know. Come back into the shtore, me tourist, and we'll see who ye shtole it from."

"Very well, officer; I can prove possession." They started back, the officer with his hand on Rowland's collar, and were met at the door by a party of three or four people coming out. One of this party, a young woman in black, uttered a piercing shriek and sprang toward them.

"Myra!" she screamed. "Give me my baby—give her to me."

She snatched the child from Rowland's shoulder, hugged it, kissed it, cried, and screamed over it; then, oblivious to the crowd that collected, incontinently fainted in the arms of an indignant old gentleman.

"You scoundrel!" he exclaimed, as he flourished his cane over Rowland's head with his free arm. "We've caught you. Officer, take that man to the station-house. I will follow and make a charge in the name of my daughter."

"Then he shtole the kid, did he?" asked the policeman.

"Most certainly," answered the old gentleman, as, with the assistance of the others, he supported the unconscious young mother to a carriage. They all entered, little Myra screaming for Rowland from the arms of a female member of the party, and were driven off.

"C'm an wi' me," uttered the officer, rapping his prisoner on the head with his club and jerking him off his feet.

Then, while an approving crowd applauded, the man who had fought and conquered a hungry polar bear was dragged through the streets like a sick animal by a New York policeman. For such is the stultifying effect of a civilized environment.

Chapter XV

In New York City there are homes permeated by a moral atmosphere so pure, so elevated, so sensitive to the vibrations of human woe and misdoing, that their occupants are removed completely from all consideration of any but the spiritual welfare of poor humanity. In these homes the news-gathering, sensation-mongering daily paper does not enter.

In the same city are dignified magistrates—members of clubs and societies—who spend late hours, and often fail to arise in the morning in time to read the papers before the opening of court.

Also in New York are city editors, bilious of stomach, testy of speech, and inconsiderate of reporters' feelings and professional pride. Such editors, when a reporter has failed, through no fault of his own, in successfully interviewing a celebrity, will sometimes send him news-gathering in the police courts, where printable news is scarce.

On the morning following the arrest of John Rowland, three

reporters, sent by three such editors, attended a hall of justice presided over by one of the late-rising magistrates mentioned above. In the anteroom of this court, ragged, disfigured by his clubbing, and disheveled by his night in a cell, stood Rowland, with other unfortunates more or less guilty of offense against society. When his name was called, he was hustled through a door, along a line of policemen—each of whom added to his own usefulness by giving him a shove—and into the dock, where the stern-faced and tired-looking magistrate glared at him. Seated in a corner of the court-room were the old gentleman of the day before, the young mother with little Myra in her lap, and a number of other ladies—all excited in demeanor; and all but the young mother directing venomous glances at Rowland. Mrs. Selfridge, pale and hollow-eyed, but happy-faced, withal, allowed no wandering glance to rest on him.

The officer who had arrested Rowland was sworn, and testified that he had stopped the prisoner on Broadway while making off with the child, whose rich clothing had attracted his attention. Disdainful sniffs were heard in the corner with muttered remarks: "Rich indeed—the idea—the flimsiest prints." Mr. Gaunt, the prosecuting witness, was called to testify.

"This man, your Honor," he began, excitedly, "was once a gentleman and a frequent guest at my house. He asked for the hand of my daughter, and as his request was not granted, threatened revenge. Yes, sir. And out on the broad Atlantic, where he had followed my daughter in the guise of a sailor, he attempted to murder that child—my grandchild; but was discovered—"

"Wait," interrupted the magistrate. "Confine your testimony to the present offense."

"Yes, your Honor. Failing in this, he stole, or enticed the little one from its bed, and in less than five minutes the ship was wrecked, and he must have escaped with the child in—"

"Were you a witness of this?"

"I was not there, your Honor; but we have it on the word of the first officer, a gentleman—"

"Step down, sir. That will do. Officer, was this offense committed in New York?"

"Yes, your Honor; I caught him meself."

"Who did he steal the child from?"

"That leddy over yonder."

"Madam, will you take the stand?"

With her child in her arms, Mrs. Selfridge was sworn and in a low, quavering voice repeated what her father had said. Being a woman, she was allowed by the woman-wise magistrate to tell her story in her own way. When she spoke of the attempted murder at the taffrail, her manner became excited. Then she told of the captain's promise to put the man in irons on her agreeing to testify against him—of the consequent decrease in her watchfulness, and her missing the child just before the shipwreck—of her rescue by the gallant first officer, and his assertion that he had seen her child in the arms of this man—the only man on earth who would harm it—of the later news that a boat containing sailors and children had been picked up by a Mediterranean steamer—of the detectives sent over, and their report that a sailor answering this man's description had refused to surrender a child to the consul at Gibraltar and had disappeared with it—of her joy at the news that Myra was alive, and despair of ever seeing her again until she had met her in this man's arms on Broadway the day before. At this point, outraged maternity overcame her. With cheeks flushed, and eyes blazing scorn and anger, she pointed at Rowland and all but screamed: "And he has mutilated—tortured my baby. There are deep wounds in her little back, and the doctor said, only last night, that they were made by a sharp instrument. And he must have tried to warp and twist the mind of my child, or put her through frightful experiences; for he has taught her to swear—horribly—and last night at bedtime, when I told her the story of Elisha and the bears and the children, she burst out into the most uncontrollable screaming and sobbing."

Here her testimony ended in a breakdown of hysterics, between sobs of which were frequent admonitions to the child not to say that bad word; for Myra had caught sight of Rowland and was calling his nickname.

"What shipwreck was this—where was it?" asked the puzzled magistrate of nobody in particular.

"The *Titan*," called out half a dozen newspaper men across the room.

"The *Titan*," repeated the magistrate. "Then this offense was committed on the high seas under the English flag. I cannot imagine why it is brought into this court. Prisoner, have you anything to say?"

"Nothing, your Honor." The answer came in a kind of dry sob.

The magistrate scanned the ashen-faced man in rags, and said to the clerk of the court: "Change this charge to vagrancy—eh—"

The clerk, instigated by the newpaper men, was at his elbow. He laid a morning paper before him, pointed to certain big letters and retired. Then the business of the court suspended while the court read the news. After a moment or two the magistrate looked up.

"Prisoner," he said, sharply, "take your left sleeve out of your breast!" Rowland obeyed mechanically, and it dangled at his side. The magistrate noticed, and read on. Then he folded the paper and said:

"You are the man who was rescued from an iceberg, are you not?" The prisoner bowed his head.

"Discharged!" The word came forth in an unjudicial roar. "Madam," added the magistrate, with a kindling light in his eye, "this man has merely saved your child's life. If you will read of his defending it from a polar bear when you go home, I doubt that you will tell it any more bear stories. Sharp instrument—umph!" Which was equally unjudicial on the part of the court.

Mrs. Selfridge, with a mystified and rather aggrieved expression of face, left the court-room with her indignant father and friends, while Myra shouted profanely for Rowland, who had fallen into the hands of the reporters. They would have entertained him after the manner of the craft, but he would not be entertained—neither would he talk. He escaped and was swallowed up in the world without; and when the evening papers appeared that day, the events of the trial were all that could be added to the story of the morning.

Chapter XVI

On the morning of the next day, a one-armed dock lounger found an old fish-hook and some pieces of string which he knotted together; then he dug some bait and caught a fish. Being hungry and without fire, he traded with a coaster's cook for a meal, and before night caught two more, one of which he traded, the other, sold. He slept under the docks—paying no rent—fished, traded, and sold for a month, then paid for a second-hand suit of clothes and the services of a barber. His changed appearance induced a boss stevedore to hire him tallying cargo, which was more lucrative than fishing, and furnished, in time, a hat, pair of shoes, and an overcoat. He then rented a room and slept in a bed. Before long he found employment addressing envelopes for a mailing firm, at which his fine and rapid penmanship secured him steady work; and in a few months he asked his employers to indorse his application for a Civil Service examination. The favor was granted, the examination easily passed, and he addressed envelopes while he waited. Meanwhile he bought new and better clothing and seemed to have no difficulty in impressing those whom he met with the fact that he was a gentleman. Two years from the time of his examination he was appointed to a lucrative position under the Government, and as he seated himself at the desk in his office, could have been heard to remark: "Now John Rowland, your future is your own. You have merely suffered in the past from a mistaken estimate of the importance of women and whisky."

But he was wrong, for in six months he received a letter which, in part, read as follows:

"Do not think me indifferent or ungrateful. I have watched from a distance while you made your wonderful fight for your old standards. You have won, and I am glad and I congratulate you. But Myra will not let me rest. She asks for you continually and cries at times. I can bear it no longer. Will you not come and see Myra?"

And the man went to see—Myra.

2

FROM THE OLD WORLD
TO THE NEW

W. T. STEAD

William Thomas Stead (1849-1912) was a flamboyant British journalist, very famous and influential in his day. As editor of the *Pall Mall Gazette* he got so carried away by his fanatical crusade against London prostitution that he lost his editorship and spent three months in prison. After leaving jail he founded the monthly *Review of Reviews,* which he edited until his death on the *Titanic.* During the Boer War he fiercely attacked his government's policies. Among his many books are such titles as *The Truth About Russia, If Christ Came to Chicago, Mrs. Booth, The Americanization of the World, Chicago Today: Or the Labor War in America, Borderland,* and *Satan's Invisible World Displayed: A Study of Greater New York.*

Like Sir Arthur Conan Doyle, Stead became an enthusiastic spiritualist. Doyle abandoned his childhood Catholicism for the new faith, but Stead, whose father was a Congregational minister, managed to combine spiritualism with a firm belief that the Bible was the word of God. He was as naive as Doyle and twice as ignorant of science and its methods. Indeed, he attacked the British Society for Psychical Research for its efforts to obtain empirical evidence! Here is how he put it in a passage that occult journalists like to cite as evidence of Stead's unconscious precognition of his death:

Stead imagined himself drowning. Instead of throwing him a rope, he pictured his would-be rescuers shouting: "Who are you? What is your name?"

"I am Stead!" he shouts back. "W. T. Stead! I am drowning here in the sea. Throw me the rope. Be quick!"

Instead of tossing the rope they continue with: "How do we know you are Stead? Where were you born? Tell us the name of your grandmother."

As for the possibility that mediums would engage in fraud, Stead said he would rather die in the workhouse than believe anyone would tell him a lie for the mere purpose of deceiving him.

Stead became a gifted automatic writer. He would pick up a pen, and his hand would be guided by telepathic communications from the unconscious minds of living persons or from the conscious minds of souls in heaven. His main spirit control was Julia Ames, a departed journalist friend who had edited the *Woman's Union Signal* in Chicago. "Mrs. Julia," in the novel from which we have taken excerpts, may have been based on Julia Ames. One of his other spirit controls— she provided Stead with political information—was Catherine II of Russia.

In 1893 Stead founded and edited *Borderland,* a quarterly journal of spiritualism, in which he published his *Letters from Julia.* These messages, received from Julia's spirit by automatic writing, were later reissued as the book *After Death.* For several years Stead maintained "Julia's Bureau," a group of mediums who met every morning to receive messages from the beyond. The mediums were selected by the spirit of Julia and included many famous sensitives of the day.

In addition to the passage quoted above about drowning, occult writers are fond of calling attention to two published works by Stead. In the *Pall Mall Gazette* in 1886 (later reprinted in *Review of Reviews,* June 1912), he wrote a story about the sinking of an ocean liner, although not as a result of hitting an iceberg, and how lives were lost because of too few lifeboats. "This is exactly what might take place," he commented, "and what will take place, if the liners are sent to sea short of boats." Needless to add, such fears were often expressed in those days, and predictions of great sea disasters were as common as predictions today about air disasters.

Stead's other instance of seeming precognition is a portion of his sentimental novel *From the Old World to the New,* in which he described the sinking of a ship in the North Atlantic after striking an iceberg. To add to the coincidence, the captain of the *Majestic,* which carries the passengers in Stead's novel, is none other than Edward J. Smith, who later became the captain of the *Titanic.*

After Stead's death, numerous psychics claimed they had warned him that he would die at sea, but evidence for all such claims is slim. In any case, Stead's beloved Julia never issued such a warning. On the contrary, Stead steadfastly believed he would die a violent death on land at the hands of a mob. "I had a vision of a mob," he wrote, "and this has made me feel that I shall not die in a way common to most of us, but by violence, and one of many in a throng." When he booked voyage on the *Titanic,* he had not the slightest premonition of disaster at sea.

No sooner had Stead entered his watery grave than mediums all over the world began getting messages from him—so many in fact that spiritualist James Coates wrote an entire book about them called *Has W. T. Stead Returned?* The most interesting case involved Mrs. Etta Wriedt, of Detroit. She was regarded by Doyle as the best "direct voice" medium in the world. Such mediums speak in voices that are close imitations of the actual voices of the dead. When Stead took the *Titanic* to New York, to make a speech about world peace at Carnegie Hall, he intended to bring Etta back to England. Two days after the *Titanic* sank, Etta's control was giving details about the disaster, and the next day Stead himself came through.

The funniest account of Stead's appearance after death can be found in Chapter 20 of *Man's Survival After Death: Or The Other Side of Life, in the Light of Scripture, Human Experience, and Modern Research.* It was first published in Edinburgh in 1909 and ran through many editions. (My 1925 copy is 536 pages.) The author, Charles L. Tweedale, was an Anglican vicar of unbounded stupidity. (Did his friends, I wonder, call him Tweedale D. D.?) He firmly believed, as did his friend Stead, that Christianity and spiritualism could travel hand in hand. On the evening after the *Titanic* sank, Tweedale tells us, after the children had been put to bed, his wife came running to him in great alarm. A man with thick eyebrows and a beard had "passed through the kitchen where she was. He had on a greyish or mixture tweed suit, with a short, round, library coat. Shortly after this, while in the kitchen, she heard wailing, crying sounds, and a kind of moaning. It sounded like *many* people in great trouble. . . ."

The next morning the Tweedales learned of the *Titanic* disaster and that Stead was lost. When Mrs. Tweedale was shown a picture of Stead, she was sure the apparition "bore a strong resemblance to him." Tweedale was absolutely convinced this was the ghost of Stead. Soon Stead was speaking to him directly in séances, in a voice that was "loud, clear, distinct and unmistakable. The evidence for the return of W. T. Stead is of the most positive kind."

Another spiritualist who believed that Stead returned through mediums was his own daughter Estelle. Her book *My Father: Personal and Spiritual Reminiscences,* is one of the major sources of information about Stead. The other is *The Life of W. T. Stead,* by William Whyte, in two volumes that are still in print in the United States in a Garland reprint of 1971.

In the first of his papers on the *Titanic,* Ian Stevenson calls attention to many inconsistencies in Stead's alleged messages through mediums. Through one sensitive he would say he went down on the *Titanic* fully conscious. Through another he would say he died in his sleep. In one séance he said it was he who asked the ship's orchestra to play "Nearer My God to Thee," but we now know this was not what the band played.

In view of his combative nature, it is not surprising that Stead was both loved and hated. Frank Harris, in his autobiography, writes of Stead: "I was rather relieved when he went down in some shipwreck and we were rid of him—just as I was glad that Bryan died . . . a disgrace to American civilization." Harris recalls an anecdote told to him by Julia Frankau, who wrote under the name of Frank Danby. She said she had flirted with Stead until one day he fell on his knees and put his arms around her. "At last!" she said to herself. To her vast amusement, as it turned out, Stead told her of his intention to pray that she would always remain faithful to her husband.

The entire Christmas issue of *Review of Reviews* in 1891 was devoted to spiritualism. For the Christmas issue of the following year Stead decided to write a novel, his first, that would introduce readers to Chicago's great World's Fair of 1893. Titled *From the Old World to the New: Or, A Christmas Story of the World's Fair, 1893* and lavishly illustrated by Arthur Twidle (no D. D.), the novel ran without a byline. Here is Stead's preface:

MOWBRAY HOUSE, *December, 1892*

The World's Fair at Chicago will be the great event of 1893. All the world and his wife will be going to the Exhibition. Few questions will be more generally discussed this Christmas at family gatherings than the attraction of the Chicago trip.

Therefore the Christmas Number of the *Review of Reviews* this year is devoted, from first page to last page, to telling the British public about Chicago and its Exhibition, and the way there.

Last year our Christmas Number, dealing with the shadowy under-world, achieved for "Real Ghosts" an unprecedented success. This year we make an equally unprecedented departure from the conventionalities of journalistic Christmasery, but we deal, not with the truth about the dim, obscure world of spirit, but with the latest embodiment of the genius, the enterprise and the labour of Man in the material realms. Yet there is a living link between the two.

Chicago Exhibition, Chicago itself—which is greater than the Exhibition, and the great Republic which welcomes all nations to the great festival of nations—these are but the latest temporary materialisation and realistic development of the great idea which possessed Columbus when, four hundred years ago, he steered his tiny caravel across the Unknown Sea and re-discovered the New World. In our last Christmas Number we collected some of the shadowy fragments of evidence as to the reality and accessibility of the Invisible World, which, however incomplete and unsatisfactory, were more numerous and more conclusive than the disjointed rumours and abstract reasonings which led the Genoese navigator to take that voyage, the fourth centenary of which is being celebrated at Chicago. Last year we indicated the New World that man has still to explore. This year we record the latest results of the supreme triumph wrested by the faith and courage of a solitary adventurer from the great mystery which had been guarded for ages by the ignorance, the timidity and the superstition of mankind.

In telling the story of the voyage of a party of English tourists from Liverpool to Chicago, the writer has endeavoured to combine two somewhat incongruous elements—the love story of the Christmas annual and the information of a guide-book. Side by side with these, in the main features of "From the Old World to the New," are incorporated two other elements, viz., a more or less dramatic representation of conclusions arrived at after twelve months' experimental study of psychical phenomena; and an exposition of the immense political possibilites that are latent in this World's Fair. To deal in a Christmas number with such practical questions as the price of tickets and the choice of hotels, and at the same time to discuss the existence of the soul after death and the prospective assumption by America of the leadership of the English-speaking race, without sacrificing the human interest of a simple story of true love, is an undertaking which might well daunt the most practised story-teller. It was necessary, therefore, to entrust the task to one who had the audacity of the novice who always believes that he can do impossibilities in his first story.

Speaking critically, as editor, of the result of this bold attempt, I may at least hazard the remark that this Christmas story deserves the compliment paid by a Scotchman to the first number of the *Review of Reviews:* "It is like a haggis—there's a good deal of confused feeding in it." I would add one other remark, viz., that I have not allowed the writer, when treating of psychometry, clairvoyancy, telepathy, or automatic handwriting, to go one step beyond the limits, not merely of the possible, but of that which has actually been attained. This I have verified by experiments conducted under conditions precluding fraud or mistake.

I wish my readers, alike in the Old World and the New, a merry Christmas and a bright New Year.

WILLIAM T. STEAD

It is a measure of Stead's skill as a journalist and researcher that he wrote this novel before making his first trip to America in the fall of 1893. Just before that trip Stead planned to launch a new daily newspaper in London, the nature of which he outlined in a supplement to the November 1893 issue of his *Review of Reviews.* Among many startling innovations, such as staffing the paper mainly with women (Stead was a dedicated feminist), he planned to publish telepathic interviews with famous people. Indeed, in the first issue he intended to run a long interview he had had with one Lady Brooke that occurred while he was on a railway carriage in Dover and Lady Brooke was at a castle in northern Scotland.

"How on earth did you accomplish this?" asked a flabbergasted reporter on the *Chicago Tribune.* (The interview appeared in the *Chicago Sunday Tribune,* November 1893). Stead replied:

"I simply took a pencil in my hand, spread a sheet of blank paper on a blotting-pad in the railway carriage, and in thought addressed Lady Brooke the questions which I should have asked her if she had been sitting on the opposite side of the carriage. Then my hand without more ado, wrote out her answer to each question. Then I asked another question and she answered it, and so on, just as if the two parties, the interviewer and the interviewed, had been face to face in the ordinary journalistic fashion. When the interview was finished I put it in my pocket, and on arriving in London an hour later, I found a letter from Lady Brooke addressed to me, which had arrived that morning. When I opened it I found it contained in brief the substance of the remarks which she had made to me, writing through my hand. When I sent a proof of the interview down to her she returned it without correction or erasure, stating that it was marvellous—the perfect accuracy with which I had tapped her mind and had succeeded in procuring a written record of her thoughts. The only criticism she had to make was that she wished I had added something more—an amplification of what she had already said. This also corresponded with my own impression, having got so sleepy from fatigue in travelling from Switzerland all night that I didn't go on with it."

"I must say, Mr. Stead, that this opens up a new and bewildering vista of journalistic possibilities."

"No doubt, I cannot say how far it may go. I do not know how long it will be before many people will write correctly through my hand. Some will not—cannot. Others scarcely ever make a mistake. If I could secure a staff of persons who were in sufficient mental *rapport* with me I would be able to have special correspondence instantaneously from the uttermost parts of the world by the simple process of letting each of them write with my hand."

It is not hard to understand why Stead failed to get financial backing for his newspaper project—a failure that was one of the great disappointments of his life.

The following pages contain a portion of Stead's novel that deals with the destruction of a ship when it rams an iceberg in the North Atlantic. To understand the excerpts it will be helpful to be familiar with the plot.

A young doctor, Walter Wynne, encounters Rose Thorne, a beautiful young woman, while visiting Ann Hathaway's Cottage in Stratford-on-Avon. The two fall instantly in love. Because she is a cottager's daughter, far below the doctor on the social scale, Rose becomes convinced she will ruin the doctor's life if she persists in seeing him. She sends him a note saying she is disappearing until "I am in a position to be loved." For years Dr. Wynne tries to locate her, but all professional efforts fail.

The doctor decides to visit the Chicago World's Fair. Improbable though it seems, he hopes he may find Rose there. At Liverpool he joins a party of English tourists who have booked passage on the White Star liner the *Majestic,* an actual ship. The principal members of the group are:

Jack Compton, a wealthy bachelor.

Professor Glogoul, a man of science. He is an atheist whose main concerns are understanding human nature and a eugenics program in which unfit babies (their unfitness determined by phrenology) will be put to death by a strong sleeping potion.

Marion Irwin, a young Irish widow. She falls in love with Compton and at the end of the story marries him.

Adelaide Julia, another beautiful young widow.

Irene Vernon. She falls in love with the professor and eventually marries him.

Mrs. Wills and her children Fred, Tom, and Pearl. She is on her way to San Francisco to meet her missionary husband.

Although the doctor never knows it, his Rose is on board the *Majestic* on a Second Class deck. Her father had been sent to Chicago to build a replica of the Ann Hathaway Cottage at the World's Fair. Mr. Thorne has taken ill, and Rose is going to see him. After she left Stratford she worked for a few years in London as a struggling artist's model before she discovered her talent for writing fantasy for children. She is now an established author who uses the name of Rose Thistle. Mrs. Julia assists Rose when she falls ill on the trip, and the two become good friends.

The episodes in the following excerpts now take place. The *Ann and Jane,* a ship running ahead of the *Majestic,* rams an iceberg in dense fog. Mrs. Irwin, a powerful psychic, has a remote vision of the three survivors in distress on the iceberg. When she tells Compton about her vision, he reveals that he has received by automatic writing, at which he is adept, a message of distress from one of the three men, John Thomas. Compton and Mrs. Irwin go to the ship's captain. Stead reproduces a drawing of Captain E. J. Smith, with a footnote saying that, although he was the real captain of the *Majestic,* the captain of his novel is imaginary. This is the very Captain Smith later to go down on the *Titanic.*

The captain is unimpressed by what he is told. Compton then has the professor hypnotize the captain's niece. In a clairvoyant state, she too sees the shipwrecked men. The captain remains skeptical, but promises to take action if the ship encounters an iceberg.

Encounter it the ship does. The professor and Compton join the men in a rescue boat. They find Thomas still alive, and with great

Sigma

R. M. S. Titanic, April 10, 1912, off the coast of France

The Veranda Café

E. J. Smith, captain of the *Titanic*

These enormous boilers for the *Titanic* crashed through the ship as it sank.

Sigma

The round capstans shown in this photograph led the Woods Hole Institute scientists to determine that this sunken ship is indeed the *Titanic*.

Morgan Robertson, author of *The Wreck of the Titan*

W. T. Stead, author of *From the Old World to the New,* went down
on the *Titanic.*

Artist: Ken Marschall

"*R. M. S. Titanic,* 11:40 P.M., April 14, 1912"

difficulty get him back to the *Majestic*. He recovers, though he may have to lose a frostbitten foot.

The *Majestic* continues on its way until it enters New York harbor. The sun's "fading rays lit up the distant spires of the Empire City. Then night fell, and the stars came out, and from the Statue of Liberty a great ribbon of electric light streamed forth over the water. It was a vestibule worthy the entrance hall of the Republic."

At New York City the travelers take trains to Chicago, but not before Stead has given a marvelous account of the city. There are even longer and better descriptions of Chicago, including colorful accounts of the Midway and the great buildings of the Fair.

Rose discovers that she too is a gifted automatic writer. She receives messages to Mrs. Julia from her dead husband, who tells her what heaven is like and how the key to everything is "love, love, love."

Rose's father, after recovering from his illness, completes the building of Ann Hathaway's Cottage in Jackson Park. Rose and the doctor are still searching desperately for each other. As providence has it, they meet in Ann's Cottage and embrace in the moonlight.

"Oh, Walter, Walter, at last, at last!" Rose exclaims with streaming eyes.

"My own Rose!" the doctor responds as the lovers hear a distant choir singing Rose's favorite hymn.

From the Old World to the New

W. T. STEAD

Coincidence and Clairvoyance

This is the last portion of Chapter 7 of W. T. Stead's novel, From the Old World to the New; or, A Christmas Story of the World's Fair, 1893.

Mr. Compton was abruptly aroused from his reverie by a direct appeal from Mrs. Irwin.

"If you have ten minutes to spare, Mr. Compton, I will be glad to have a word with you by yourself."

"Certainly, madam, will you come to the Library? It is sure to be empty just now, and we can speak at leisure."

They soon found themselves ensconced in a corner of the Library. There were only one or two ladies present, and shortly afterwards these left Compton and Mrs. Irwin alone.

"I would not have ventured to trouble you," said Mrs. Irwin, "but I know that you are no stranger to occult things. If I had not seen that in the face of you I should not have ventured to speak."

"Yes, yes," said Compton, somewhat impatiently, "but what has that to do with it?"

"It has everything to do with it, sir," said she; "because, if you did not understand, it would be no use trying to explain. I must tell you that I come of one of the oldest families in Ireland. We have the Banshee, of course, but, what is more to the purpose, I have occasionally the gift of second sight. Now, last night—"

Compton, who at first had listened with hardly concealed impatience, suddenly manifested eager interest.

"My dear Mrs. Irwin," he exclaimed, "why did you not tell me this before? Nothing interests me so much as to come upon those rare but peculiarly gifted persons who have inherited, or acquired by some strange gift of the gods, the privilege—often a sombre and terrible privilege—of seeing into futurity."

"Sombre and terrible you may well say it is," said Mrs. Irwin, "and fain would I be without it. It is a gruesome thing to see, as I have done, the funeral in the midst of the wedding-feast, and to mark the shroud high on the breast of the heir when he comes of age. But the gift comes when it comes, and goes when it goes; it seems as fitful as the shooting-stars which come no one knows from whence, and disappear no one knows whither."

"Well," said Compton, "you were saying that last night—?"

"I was saying," said Mrs. Irwin, "that last night, as I was lying asleep in my berth, I was awakened by a sudden cry, as of men in mortal peril, and I roused myself to listen, and there before my eyes, as plain as you are sitting there, I saw a sailing ship among the icebergs. She had been stove in by the ice, and was fast sinking. The crew were crying piteously for help: it was their voices that roused me. Some of them had climbed upon the ice; others were on the sinking ship, which was drifting away as she sank. Even as I looked she settled rapidly by the bow, and went down with a plunge. The waters bubbled and foamed. I could see the heads of a few swimmers in the eddy. One after another they sank, and I saw them no more. I saw that there were six men and a boy on the iceberg. Then, in a moment, the whole scene vanished, and I was alone in my berth, with the wailing cry of the drowning sailors still ringing in my ears."

"Did you notice the appearance of any of the survivors?" said he, anxiously.

"As plainly as I am looking at you," she replied. "I noticed especially one man, very tall—over six feet, I should say—who wore a curious Scotch plaid around his shoulders and a Scotch cap on his head. He had a rough red beard, and one eye was either blind or closed up."

"And did you see the name of the ship before it foundered?"

"Certainly I did; it was plain to see as it went down headforemost. I read the name on the stern. It was the *Ann and Jane* of Montrose."

Compton rose from his chair, and took a turn or two in deep thought. Then he stopped, and said,—

"Mrs. Irwin, you have trusted me, I will trust you. What you said has decided me, or rather has given me hope that we may be able to induce the captain of the *Majestic* to rescue these unfortunates, one of whom is a friend of my own."

"But did you know about it before I spoke?" asked Mrs. Irwin.

"I need not explain to you," said Compton, not heeding the interruption, "for you understand that there is no impossibility in the instantaneous communication of intelligence, from any distance, to others who have what some have described as the sixth sense. To some it comes in the form of clairvoyance, to others as clairaudience, while to a third class, among whom I count myself, it comes in the shape of what is called automatic writing. I have many friends in all parts of the world who also have this gift, and we use it constantly, to the almost entire disuse of the telegraph. At least once every day, each of us is under a pledge to place his hand at the disposal of any of the associated friends who may wish urgently to communicate with him. This morning, at noon, when I placed my hand with the pen on my dispatch book, it wrote off, with feverish rapidity, a message which I will now read to you:

"'John Thomas. Tuesday morning, four o'clock. The *Ann and Jane*, Montrose, struck on an iceberg in the fog in North Atlantic, and almost immediately foundered. Six men and a boy succeeded in reaching the ice alive. All others were drowned. For God's sake, rescue us speedily; otherwise death is certain from cold and hunger. We are close to the line of outward steamers.—John Thomas.'

"The signature, you see," said Compton, "is the same as that appended to the last letter I received from him, which I hunted up after I had received this message. I have, therefore, no doubt that 'John Thomas' with five other men and a boy are exposed to a lingering death on the iceberg some hundred miles ahead."

"But," said Mrs. Irwin, "what can we do?"

"That," replied Compton, "is my difficulty. To have gone to the captain with this message, without any confirmation but my word, would probably have exposed me to certain ridicule, and might have led the captain to steer still further to the south. Now, however, that you also have had the message, I will hesitate no longer."

Without more ado, he wrote a short note to the captain, begging to be allowed to communicate with him on a matter of urgent and immediate importance, involving questions of life and death.

Hardly had the messenger departed with the note when the professor and the doctor entered the library.

"Halloo, Compton," said the professor, "are you not coming on deck to see the fog? But, in the name of fortune, what is the matter? Doctor, I think you had better look to Compton."

"It's nothing," said Compton faintly, "only a passing qualm. Is the fog very dense?"

"You can see it in the distance like a dim grey wall lying right across the bows of the steamer. We shall be into it in half-an-hour. But," persisted the professor, "something is up. Can I not help?"

"Professor," said Compton, a sudden thought striking him, "if I send for you from the captain's cabin, please hold yourself in readiness to come."

"Certainly," said the professor. "But what, in the name of commonsense, are you troubling the captain for just as the ship is entering an ice fog?"

"Mr. Compton, the captain will see you at once in the cabin," said the returned messenger.

"Now, Mrs. Irwin; not one word to any one! Professor, I may send for you shortly."

So saying, he followed the messenger to the captain's cabin. It is but seldom that any passenger ventures to intrude into that sanctum. But Mr. Compton was not an ordinary passenger. He had often crossed the Atlantic in vessels under the command of the present captain. He was known to be a man of power, of influence, and of wealth. More than that, he had, on more than one occasion, given invaluable information, procured no one knew how or where, which had enabled the captain to avoid imminent dangers into which he was steaming at full speed. He was, therefore, assured of a respectful hearing, even from the autocrat of the *Majestic* on the verge of an ice fog.

"Now, Mr. Compton," said the captain,* "what is it you wish to say to me? I have only a few minutes to spare. We shall have to steer Southward to avoid the ice floe which is drifting across our usual course."

*I need not say that the whole of this story is purely imaginary. Although I illustrate the account of the voyage with a portrait of the real captain of the *Majestic*, he must not be in any way identified with the captain of this story.

"I want you," said Mr. Compton, imperturbably, "to continue your usual course in order to pick up six men and a boy, who are stranded on an iceberg from the ship *Ann and Jane,* of Montrose, which foundered at four o'clock this morning, after collision with the ice."

The captain stared. "Really, Mr. Compton, how do you know that? It is impossible for any one to know it."

Mr. Compton replied. "There is the despatch from one of my friends, John Thomas, who was on the ship, and is now on the iceberg, received by me in his own handwriting at noon this day."

The captain took the paper with an uneasy expression of countenance.

"Entering the fog, sir," said an officer, putting his head into the cabin.

"Slacken speed," said the captain. "I shall be out in a moment."

He carefully read and re-read the paper, and then said—

"Well, really, if you were not Mr. Compton I should consider you a lunatic. What possible reliance can be placed upon such a statement?"

"I received this," replied Compton, significantly, "in the same way that I received the message of 1889, which enabled you to—"

"I remember," said the captain; "otherwise, I should not be listening to you now."

"But this story has not come without confirmation;" and then Compton repeated Mrs. Irwin's clairvoyant vision.

"What do I care for these old women's stories," said the captain. "But even if they were true, what then? I have nearly 2,000 passengers and crew, all told, on board the *Majestic.* I dare not risk them and the ship, hunting for a half-dozen castaways on an iceberg on the North Atlantic."

"But," said Compton, "if you are convinced that the men are there, dare you leave them to their fate?"

"But I am not convinced. They may have died ere now, even if they ever were there at all."

"Might I ask you to give me a pencil and paper," said Compton.

The captain handed him what he wanted. Compton at once grasped the pencil, and placed it on the paper. Almost immediately it wrote:—

"John Thomas. Iceberg. Three o'clock. At one o'clock the iceberg parted under our feet, three men and a boy were carried away. Three still remain, frost bitten, without food or fire. We shall not be able to survive the night. When the *Ann and Jane* foundered, we were on the outward liners' route, 45 by 45, on the extreme southern edge of the ice-floe. Since then, it has rather receded. For God's sake, do not desert us.—John Thomas."

The captain stared at the curious writing, which was not Compton's, and then stared at Compton.

The latter merely said, "How far are we off the position mentioned?"

The captain looked at the chart.

"We are steering by our present altered course directly upon the spot where he says the berg is floating. If I believed your message, I would steer still more to the southward, to give the ice a clear berth. It is no joke shaving round an iceberg in such a fog as this. But I do not believe your message, and I will not alter the course of the *Majestic* by one point, for all the witches and wizards that ever lived."

"Captain," said Compton, "your niece is on board, I believe?"

"Yes," said the captain. "But what in the world has she to do with it?"

"If you will allow her to come here, and permit me to send for my friend, the professor, I think we shall be able to convince you that these sailors are waiting deliverance."

The captain rang the bell. "Bring my niece here instantly," he said, "and Professor Glogoul. Thank heaven," he added, "the fog is so dense, no one will be able to see them come, or else they would think—and think rightly—that I had taken leave of my wits."

In a minute or two, the niece and the professor had both arrived.

"Captain," said Compton, "will you let your niece sit down? The professor hypnotized her in a previous voyage, and cured her of seasickness. He can cast her into hypnotic sleep with her consent, by merely making a pass over her face with his hand."

The captain growled, "Do what you like, only make haste. If it were any one but Mr. Compton," he muttered under his breath, "if it were any one but Mr. Compton, I should very soon have cleared the cabin."

The captain's niece had hardly taken her seat when the professor's pass threw her into a hypnotic sleep. A few more passes and the professor said she was in the clairvoyant state.

"What is it that you want?" he asked.

"Tell her," said Compton, "to go ahead of the ship in the exact course she is now steering, and tell us what she sees."

The professor repeated the request. Almost immediately the captain's niece began to shiver and shudder, then she spoke—

"I go on for half-an-hour, then for an hour; it gets colder and colder. I see ice, not icebergs, but floating ice. I go through this floating ice for an hour, for two hours, then the fog gets thinner and thinner, it almost disappears. I see icebergs, they shine beautifully in the sunlight. There are many of them stretching for miles and miles, as far as I can see. What a noise there is when they break and capsize."

"Do you see any ship or any thing?" asked the professor.

"No, I see nothing, only icebergs. I go on and on for another hour. Then I see on an iceberg, near the foot, some one making signals. I come nearer, I see him plainly. It is a tall man with one eye and red hair. He is walking up and down. Beside him there is one man sitting, and another man who seems to be dead. It seems to be the edge of the iceberg. There is clear water beyond."

"That will do," said Compton.

The professor blew lightly on the girl's face.

She opened her eyes, and stood up looking round with a dazed expression.

"Well," said Compton to the captain, "are you convinced?"

"Convinced!" said the captain. "It's all confounded nonsense. Out with you! If you ever had to steer the *Majestic* through an ice fog in the mid-Atlantic you would know better than to fool away the captain's time by such a pack of tomfoolery."

The niece and the professor left the cabin.

As Compton turned to go he said, "Captain, that tall, one-eyed man on the iceberg is one of my friends. You will keep on your course, as you say:—I desire nothing better. Will you promise me, if only for the sake of the past, that if you strike drift-ice in an hour and a half, and if you emerge from the fog two hours later on the edge of the floe of icebergs, you will keep a look-out and save John Thomas if you can?"

"If, if, if," said the captain, contemptuously. "Oh, yes, if all these things happen, I will promise; never fear, I can safely promise that!"

As Compton left the cabin the captain remarked—

"They say it is always the cleverest men who have got the biggest bee in their bonnet, and upon my word I begin to believe it."

The Castaways

Chapter 8 of Stead's novel.

When Compton left the captain's cabin he felt a spring of exhilaration. The very incredulity, the natural and proper incredulity of the captain, would lead directly to the result which he desired. He would save his friend. The chances against it seemed a million to one—to pick up a castaway on an iceberg, the exact location of which was uncertain, and which might be anywhere within fifty or five hundred miles. What seemed more utterly hopeless! But Compton had seen too much of the marvellous perception of clairvoyant subjects under hypnotism to doubt that, if the captain only kept on the southward course, which he had marked out in order to avoid the floe, the rescue would certainly take place.

Mentally transmitting a telepathic message to his friend on the iceberg, fearing greatly that he would not be able to receive it owing to the difficulty, if not impossibility, of practising automatic handwriting on the shifting ice, Compton made his way through the fog to his cabin, where he found the professor waiting him.

"Well," said that worthy, "what is it all about? It is rather unusual to summon one to an experiment when the experimenter is kept so totally in the dark."

Compton soon satisfied the curiosity of the professor, and sent him to tell the doctor and Mrs. Irwin and the captain's niece what had happened. He then sat down in his berth with his dispatch book open before him and pencil in hand awaiting the arrival of further messages from the iceberg.

Meanwhile, the steamer was forging her way onward through the fog. The passengers were either in their berths or in the saloon, or the smoking-room. None were on deck. Mrs. Wills and Mrs. Julia were with Rose in her cabin. The doctor had undertaken to look after the boys and Pearl. Irene was looking out for the professor, whom she soon discovered, not at all to her satisfaction, in close conversation with Mrs. Irwin. Somehow or other, she did not like that Irishwoman, and every minute Dr. Glogoul remained with her the more she felt that Mrs. Irwin was the most objectionable of her sex.

The dense, cold fog filled the air. You breathed it and swallowed it, and saw dimly through it across the saloon. On deck all was strained attention. The captain on the bridge kept constant look out, bearing upon his shoulders the responsibility for 2,000 lives, and a ship with cargo worth at least nearly £400,000. The quartermaster outside the pilot house passed in the commands given by the captain to the first officer and to his messmate at the wheel. Every half-minute the fog whistle boomed its great voice into the fog. Sometimes, as from a far away distance, they heard the boom of another fog horn, but they could see nothing. At the bows, the deck look-out peered into the impenetrable mist; and the quartermaster posted to the leeward, and lowered the thermometer in a little canvass bag to test the temperature of the sea in hopes of timely warning of the coming ice.

The boys cowered close to the doctor, and asked him endless questions about the fog.

"Where does it come from? Who made it? What was the good of it? How could they sail through it without being able to see the end of the ship?"

"This fog," replied the doctor, "came from icebergs."

But that opened up another range of questions.

"What were icebergs? Where did they come from? Would there be bears upon them?" And so forth. A sharp child will ask more questions in ten minutes than a clever man can answer in an hour.

"Icebergs," said the doctor, "are mountains of ice floating about in the sea. Ice, you know, does not sink in water. The bergs float just a little above the surface. All the rest is below. These icebergs are born in Greenland. The snow falls on the high land, and as it does not melt, and ever more and more snow falls, the great mass presses the lowest snow downwards and ever downwards to the sea. Thus glaciers are formed, slowly-moving solid rivers of frozen and solidified snow. When the glacier pushes its way into the sea, its end breaks off, tumbles over into the water with a noise like thunder, and becomes an iceberg. The glaciers are constantly making icebergs. These icebergs drift slowly away into the sea. Sometimes they get caught by the frost, and are winterbound. When summer comes, they drift off again into the current which carries them southward. A whole archipelago of icebergs will sometimes sail southward right across the ocean route to America."

"Isn't it very dangerous?" asked Tom.

"It is the greatest danger of the voyage. For the icebergs bring fogs with them, and the fogs hide the icebergs until the steamer is close upon them. Imagine a country as big as Ireland without lighthouses, foghorns, or any beacons, suddenly towed across the path of the steamer, and then enveloped in this dense frost-fog, and you can imagine. Hark, what is that?"

There was a sound as if the steamer were crashing through ice, and the screws were churning away amid the ice blocks. The doctor ran out to see what was the matter.

When he was gone, Tom said to Fred, "It is very terrible and cold. Are you not afraid?"

"Rather," said Fred. "I wish mother were here. Are you frightened, Pearl?"

"No, I is not," said the little lady, with emphasis, "and Kitty is not frightened either."

"But, Pearl," said Fred. "the fog—"

Pearl interrupted him disdainfully. "Can't God see in the fog, Fred?"

The conversation was interrupted by the doctor's return.

"It is not icebergs, boys. It is only the floe ice which the great ship goes through as Tom here goes through sugar candy."

"What is floe ice, doctor?" asked Fred.

"Loose drift ice, formed in winter off Labrador and Newfoundland. It is not dangerous. It is only icebergs that are dangerous."

"Do ships ever run against icebergs, doctor?" said Tom.

"Oh, yes, about four are lost every year in that way. But even if we did strike an iceberg, we probably should not sink. The *Arizona* once went full speed into an iceberg, and crumpled up thirty feet of her nose. She did not sink, but got safely to Newfoundland. I hope, however, we shall not try a similar experiment."

"Doctor," said little Pearl, "could you go to find mamma?"

"Certainly, Pearl," said the doctor, "and where must I look for her?"

Tom replied, "She went with Mrs. Julia to see the sick lady in the second class. I think I can take you there if you will take my hand."

"All right, Tom," said the doctor, cheerily, "I can leave Pearl with you, Fred, till we come back. Ta-ta."

They felt their way cautiously to the deck. It was wet and clammy and bitterly cold. Every half minute the fog whistle blew: the clashing of the floe ice against the sides of the ship, and the champing of the ice under the screws made it difficult to speak so as to be heard. Tom, however, felt his way along to the second class cabin where he had left his mother an hour before with Mrs. Julia. The doctor knocked at the door.

"Hush," said Mrs. Wills, as she came out, "the poor girl is asleep." She pointed to the upper berth. His eyes dazzled by the sudden glare of the electric light, saw nothing clearly beyond a prostrate form under the rug.

"Good-evening, Mrs. Julia," said he, "I have come for Mrs. Wills. Pearl has sent me to bring her along."

There was a slight movement in the upper berth. "I'd better go at once," said Mrs. Wills, "she is stirring," and so saying, she closed the door, and the three made the best of their way back to the saloon.

Half-an-hour later, Rose awoke. "Adelaide," she murmured. Mrs. Julia reached up, and kissed her. As she did so, she saw a strange light in her face, a kind of radiance that was heightened rather than diminished by the tears that filled her eyes.

"Adelaide," she said, "I have seen him! He has been here."

"Nonsense, child," said Mrs. Julia. "You have been dreaming. I never left you since you fell asleep."

"You may not have seen him," said Rose, calmly. "I did. I cannot be mistaken. I heard his voice, that voice which I have never heard from his lips for seven long years, but which I have never ceased to hear in my dreams. I heard his voice quite distinctly. I looked up, and there he was standing, older than when I knew him, with a sadder, more wistful look than he had in the old days. But it was he."

"My dear child," said Mrs. Julia, authoritatively, "you must have been dreaming. Your illness has made you a little light in your head. I assure you, I have been here the whole time, and except Mr. Vernon, who came to bring Mrs. Wills to her children, not a living soul has entered the cabin."

"Adelaide," she replied, "I am too weak to argue. You may not have seen him. I did. He is on the ship. I know it. You cannot deceive me."

Mrs. Julia saw it was indeed no use arguing. So, bidding her lie quite still and take a good dinner, she departed.

All this while Mr. Compton was in the cabin, watching the movements of his hand, as a telegraphist watches the movements of the needle. It wrote a good deal. Messages were written out, and signed by telepathic friends in Melbourne, London, and Chicago. Then came the writing as before.

"John Thomas. Iceberg, 4.0. Are you coming? We cannot hold out much longer. One of the men is too frost-bitten to move. The fog is clearing.—John Thomas."

Then came more messages from Edinburgh, the Cape, and Singapore. It was singular to note the confidence with which correspondents in such distant regions communicated with their chief in mid-Atlantic. But he had only eyes for one correspondent. At half-past four, it wrote again.—

"John Thomas. Iceberg, 4.30. The fog has gone. The sun is shining. We are on the outer edge of the iceberg field. If you skirt it, you cannot fail to see us—unless the iceberg falls over again. The frost-bitten man is dead. We can hold out till sunset—no later.—John Thomas."

Again more messages from other correspondents, which his hand wrote out without his eye following the lines. At half-past five came the writing.—

"John Thomas. Iceberg, 5.30. I cannot now see the time. My companion can no longer keep his feet. My strength is failing.—John Thomas."

Compton could stand it no longer. Closing his dispatch-book, he hurried upon deck. He saw and heard the floe ice, and it seemed to him that the fog was not so dense. He saw the captain on the bridge. He went forward where the look-out was keeping a sharp look out on the deck. Suddenly he heard the cry,—

"Icebergs on the starboard."

The captain shouted something inaudible in the crash of the ice, the engine bell rang, the engines slowed down their speed, the steamer steered a trifle more to the southward, but still kept pounding her way onward. He could only see ghastly shadows looming darkly to the northward. If his friend was on one of these phantasmal masses, what hope was there? Sick at heart he sought out Mrs. Irwin.

"Should you know the iceberg which you saw in your vision if you saw it again?"

"Certainly, I would," she replied. "It was very irregular, with huge overhanging pinnacles. I could swear to it among a thousand."

"Stand here, then, near the deck look-out, and keep your eye fixed on the north. It may be that the mist will rise."

He went back to his cabin. The professor was awaiting him.

"Well?" said he.

"It is not well," groaned Compton. As he opened his dispatch-book to see if any fresh message was waiting to be taken down, his hand wandered a little over the paper. Then it began;—

"John Thomas. Iceberg. My companion is dead. I am alone on the iceberg. I can no longer stand or walk. In another hour all will be over.—John Thomas."

"Halloo!" said the professor. "The fog has lifted!"

Compton rushed from the cabin, and tore madly to the bridge, where the captain was standing.

"Captain," he cried, "remember your promise!"

And as he spake, he pointed to a great flotilla of icebergs. Behind the steamer the fog was as thick as a blanket. Before her was open water. On the north stretched the dazzling array of icebergs, ever shifting and moving. Now and again a great berg would capsize with a reverberant roar. The captain was cowed. There was something un-canny and awesome about the incident. He had seen icebergs before, but he had seldom had such good luck as to pass clear by the southern edge of the floe, and then to have clear sky.

He sent for Mr. Compton to the bridge.

"Captain," said Compton, before the other had time to speak, "remember your promise. Here we are in open water outside the fog, just off the southern edge of the icebergs. Will you save John Thomas?"

The captain shrugged his shoulders. "How do I know where he is? Am I to use the *Majestic,* with 2,000 souls on board, to go hunting for John Thomas among that wilderness of icebergs? Ask yourself, Is it reasonable?"

Compton replied, "If I am able to point out the exact iceberg where John Thomas lies, will you stop and send a boat to bring him aboard?"

"Yes," said the captain, "I could not well refuse that."

The *Majestic* was now driving ahead at full speed. All the passengers were on deck enjoying the novel and magnificent spectacle. Suddenly a cry was heard from the bows. It was a woman's voice, shrill and piercing.

"There it is! That is it! That is the iceberg!"

A rush was made forward. Mrs. Irwin was carried to the captain. Then she said: "We are abreast of it, and will be past it in a minute. Oh, stop her, for the Lord's mercy! You are not going to leave three men to die?"

The captain took no notice, but keenly scrutinised through his glasses the peculiar-shaped iceberg which she indicated. "'Tis curious," he muttered. "I seem to see a speck of something on the base of that berg."

The bell in the engine-room sounded, the engines stopped, and the great steamer, for the first time since leaving Queenstown, came to a standstill.

The ship was full of buzzing comments and eager inquiry. Why had the engines been stopped? What was the matter? Never was such a thing heard of—to bring to off an ice floe. There was now very little floating ice. The sea was tranquil. But who could say how soon the fog might fall again, or the northern bergs drift across the ship's route? The captain must be mad? Was there an accident in the engine-room? No, nothing was wrong there. What then? In that hubbub the voices of those who held the highest numbers in the pool were loudest in angry denunciation of the captain.

And in all this hubbub where was Compton? In his cabin, eagerly deciphering the words which his hand wrote, hardly being able to do so for the tears which blinded him. It wrote:

"John Thomas. Iceberg. I am dying. I have lost all use of my limbs. I can see a steamer in the distance, but it will not stop. I cannot make any signal. Good-bye, chief; good-bye.—John Thomas."

While he was deciphering this in his cabin, the crew, by the captain's orders, were busily engaged in lowering one of the ship's boats. A whisper ran through the ship that there was a castaway on one of the icebergs, and in a moment everyone on board, excepting the holders of the larger numbers, was intensely interested, and even enthusiastic.

Compton came up to the captain. "Captain," he said "I am afraid it is too late, but grant me one favour?"

"Well?"

"Let the professor and me go in the boat. My friend cannot help himself. He is motionless and frost-bitten. Someone must climb the iceberg. It is not a task his friends should throw upon others. The professor and I are ready."

The captain said "Go."

The boat was now launched, the men were at the oars, when the professor and Mr. Compton, carrying ice axes, a rope ladder, a coil of rope, and a bag with brandy and other restoratives, climbed down the side of the ship and took their seats.

How the passengers cheered as they rowed away; cheered, too, in spite of the angry order to desist lest the sound should disturb the very slender equilibrium of some floating mountain.

They were about a mile from the iceberg. The officer in command of the boat conferred with Mr. Compton, who briefly explained what was to be done.

As the boat approached the iceberg, they could distinctly see three bodies, but they could make out no signs of life.

Nearer and nearer they rowed, cautiously but boldly, although every now and then huge blocks of ice detached themselves from the berg, and fell with ominous crash into the water.

Nearer still and nearer the boat rowed, until it was almost within a stone's-throw of the iceberg. Then Compton, standing up, hailed his friend. There was a dull echo from the perpendicular ice-cliff, but the silent, motionless figures made no sign.

"Too late, I fear," muttered Compton through his clenched teeth. "Never mind, let us bring him to the ship, dead or alive."

The three bodies were lying on a ledge about twenty feet above the level of the water. When the berg had split, the portion that broke off was that which had afforded the crew a tolerably easy landing-stage. Now there seemed nothing for it but for the boat to lay up alongside the steep ice-wall, and for the rescue party to climb aloft as best they could.

Then another difficulty revealed itself. The sloping ice stretched under water for some twenty or thirty yards, so that the boat could not draw up to the face of the ledge.

"There is nothing for it," said Compton, "but for you to pull on until you feel the ice beneath your keel; then the professor and I will wade to the face of the cliff, and climb up."

The boat soon bumped on the ice. Compton got out into the water first, followed by the professor. The latter insisted upon carrying some strange machine round his waist. Each had an axe, and they carried with them a rope-ladder, a small coil of rope, and a flask of brandy. They got out cautiously, fearing lest a sudden spring might possibly bring the whole mountain down upon their heads. In that case, not only were the boat's crew doomed, but even the *Majestic,* a mile away, might be in danger.

They imagined they felt the ice give a little under the water, but they ignored it, and were soon at the foot of the ledge on which lay three motionless figures.

Compton and the professor were experienced mountaineers. They had little difficulty in cutting steps, on which they could climb, but the ice was rotten, and often gave way beneath their tread. On one occasion Compton, who was leading, came down with a heavy crash on the professor, laming his left shoulder. They began again at a place where the ice seemed more solid. This time Compton went up alone.

The moment he gained the ledge, an enthusiastic cheer went up from the *Majestic,* where his every movement was followed with breathless interest. Compton went directly to the longest of the prostrate forms.

"John Thomas," he said.

There was no answer. He laid his hand upon his face; it was all frost-bitten, and as if it were dead.

"Too late!" he muttered; "too late!"

The professor's head was just appearing above the ledge, when a heavy boulder, so to speak, of ice fell with a sullen crash out to the sea, dangerously jeopardising the safety of the boat.

"I am afraid it is too late," said Compton, sullenly.

The professor stepped blithely to the side of the apparent corpse.

"No," said he; "you will see the use of my patent galvano-vitalizer."

He undid the machine he carried round his waist, and uncoiled some wires, to which plates of copper were attached. One he placed at the back of the neck, the other on the abdomen. Then he proceeded to turn a handle.

"Sit by his head, Compton," he said, "and if he shows any signs of reviving, give him a small mouthful of brandy."

For a time it seemed as if the handle might be turned for ever without producing more effect upon the body than upon the ice on which it lay. But after a while the apparent corpse began to twitch, the eyelids began to move, and then the mouth opened, and a heavy sigh told that vitality had been restored.

Compton tried, at first in vain, to pour some brandy down his throat. It only choked him, and it almost seemed as if John Thomas had survived the cold only to be killed by restoratives. At last, however, they got him sufficiently revived to get him to swallow some spirit, and to take a spoonful of strong beef-tea.

The professor then took off the galvano-vitalizer, and proceeded to fasten the rope-ladder down the side of the cliff. He fixed the two ice-axes securely in the ice, and slung the ladder over the edge. He then fastened the small cord round John Thomas's waist. Compton and he carried the half-senseless, frost-bitten man to the top of the ladder. The professor then descended until he was in a position to take John Thomas's legs on his shoulders. He then began slowly to descend, Compton relieving him of as much of the weight as possible by means of the cord. By this means they got safely down to the water, and from thence it was comparatively easy to carry him to the boat. The professor was just returning for the ice-axes, the rope-ladder, and, above all, for his admirable galvano-vitalizer, when a cry was raised in the boat which made his blood run cold—

"The fog! the fog!"

Looking round, he saw that the fog was sweeping over the sea, and the outline of the *Majestic* could hardly be distinguished. Another ten minutes they might not be able to find their way back. The professor forgot even his machine and leapt into the boat. The men bent to their oars as for life, and sent the boat flying over the water like a bird.

Denser and denser grew the fog, but they could see the *Majestic* right before them, and in another moment they were alongside. Just as they reached the ship they heard a long roar like the reverberation of a park of artillery, and then the water heaved violently and dashed the boat heavily against the side of the *Majestic*.

There was a moment of agonising suspense. No one knew whether the displacement in the iceberg might not lead to a sudden upheaval of an iceberg under the keel of the *Majestic*. There was a deathly silence. Then the water began to subside, and the boat's crew, with Compton and the professor, and the frozen, half-dead survivor were brought safely to deck.

There was too much alarm about the fog for much demonstration of enthusiasm. But, when the engines were once more started, and the *Majestic* felt her way slowly through the fog to the clear waters beyond, there was not one passenger on board who did not feel glad that the liner had laid to for two whole hours to save that one miserable castaway.

But there were some on board who were filled with deeper feelings than those of mere admiration and sympathy. During the whole of the two hours they had been absent from the ship Irene had watched their progress with a strained interest of emotion which left her no room even for the thought that she was experiencing the most terrible thrill of her life. She had hurriedly thrown an old waterproof over her dinner dress, and stood against the bulwarks following through the glass every movement of the professor, for it was he and he alone for whom she cared. She feared he did not care much for her. Why should he? She was but a silly girl with a pretty face. He was one of the greatest scientists of the world. She would rather be trampled on by him than be made love to by all the other men in the ship. She had always been piqued by his impersonal method of regarding her as alkali capable of yielding certain results when tested with acids; and she was honestly dazzled by his learning and genius, but this excursion of his to the iceberg suddenly transformed him into the prince and hero of her dreams. None of the other men in the boat, not even Compton, seemed to be worth a thought. The professor, and he alone, was the hero-leader of the expedition. How noble he seemed! His very eye seemed to glow with divine light as the boat left the ship. That he seemed supremely indifferent to her only added to his charm.

From all which meditations it may be inferred that Irene was experiencing for the first time an entirely new sensation of utter humility and of self-effacement. As the boat lessened in the distance, she had kept her glass fixed upon the professor, following him with an emotion too deep for utterance until he landed below the ice ledge.

An indefinable feeling of horror came over her as she saw he was in the water. She watched them cutting steps in the ice; but her indignation knew no bounds when she saw Compton go up first. What effrontery to thrust himself before her hero! But when, just as Compton was nearing the top, his foothold gave way he fell heavily upon the professor below, both falling into the water, it seemed to her as if she were witnessing a murder. In that one terrible moment the flame of her love and her life seemed to flare up with one fierce spasm and then go out for ever in horrible darkness of nothingness and despair. She gave a piteous scream. Her glass dropped from her hands over the bulwarks into the water, and she fell swooning on the deck. So great was the excitement at the moment that she lay for some minutes unnoticed. Then the doctor and one of the stewards carried her to the saloon, where they applied restoratives. She lay quite insensible, but as she was breathing heavily and evenly, they left her, and returned to watch the attempt at rescue.

There was another spectator who was only one degree less interested than Irene. That was Mrs. Irwin. She had been deeply impressed by the straightforward manliness of Mr. Compton, and attracted to him by his occult gifts. The incident of the wreck off the iceberg established a sympathy between them, and she felt naturally intensely interested in the rescue of the tall, red-haired, one-eyed man whom she had seen more than twelve hours before when they must have been distant nearly 200 miles. She would have gladly gone in the boat, but it was idle proposing it. So she had perforce prepared to choose the more arduous task of watching while Compton risked his life to save the castaway.

Mrs. Irwin was of a practical nature amid all her dreams and mystic imaginings. She did not merely watch, she prayed, prayed with all the intensity of a passionate nature for the safety of the man for whom alone she felt reviving in her breast the stormy emotions that she believed had been hushed for ever in her husband's grave. "Something had gone snap inside," she used to say, "when she heard the clods fall on the coffin lid." She could never feel again as she felt in the glad old days when she wandered with her lover under the olive trees of the Riviera, or sat on the promontory rock of Monaco, and saw in the cool of the night the great moon shine double in sky and sea. All was dust and ashes within, and yet she felt, almost with a sense of profanation, the quickening throb of the old emotion as she watched Mr.

Compton climb up the ice cliff. When he fell she cried, "O God, let it be the other one!" for her quick nature never hesitated a moment to sacrificing the professor or a hecatomb of professors to save Compton. She felt as if her prayer was granted when Compton struggled to his feet and the professor rose rubbing his shoulder. Every step up the cliff was accompanied by passionate prayer, the outpourings of a woman's will, so potent often for ill as to justify the witch's tar-barrel, but this time employed to bless, not to curse.

The moment she saw them reach the boat in safety, and pull off through the mist, her practical common-sense asserted itself. She bustled to the steward and made him prepare the most commodious berth in the ship for the reception of John Thomas, supply warm blankets, and provide all manner of creature comforts. She brought out the steward of Mr. Compton's cabin, and induced him to provide plenty of warmed wraps, and the doctor got ready every kind of medicament and cordial.

When Compton stepped on board the ship, the impulsive Irish woman seized his hand with both of hers, and exclaimed:

"Mr. Compton, Mr. Compton! the Lord reward you for this day."

He looked up at her glowing face and sparkling eyes, from which her whole soul was beaming in admiration and worship, and then moved slowly towards his berth without saying a word. She accompanied him with the doctor. When he reached the door, he said:

"It was a very near thing, Mrs. Irwin, nearer than I ever care to be in again. I am faint. The doctor will look after me. Good-night."

She seized his proffered hand, wrung it passionately, and rushed away.

"Doctor," said Compton, slowly, "undress me, and let me sleep."

The doctor undressed him, but did not let him sleep. He chafed his frozen hands, plied him with strong and heated cordials, and made him drink a cup of the best clear soup the cook could provide, and then, when at last after an hour spent in this way he was allowed to sleep, all danger was passed.

As for John Thomas, he was cared for by the ship's doctor. With skilful treatment and constant care life began to return, and by the morning he could speak.

As for the professor, he slipped away in the confusion, and was making his way through the saloon to his berth when he was startled by seeing Irene, her long black hair streaming behind, her face pallid as death, her eyes swollen, her whole appearance that of one almost distraught. She did not seem to see him, but moved as if she were in a dream. They were in a narrow corridor where two could pass with difficulty. He was obliged to speak; all wet as he was he could not allow her to spoil her dress. "Miss Vernon," he said, "do you not see me?"

She gave a frightened cry, turned to run, with horror on her countenance.

The professor sighed for his cunning little instrument which measured emotion, and then, before Irene had time to run two steps, he caught her hand.

"Miss Vernon, this is a poor welcome," he said.

Irene stopped instantly, turned, and regarded him intently.

"Then—you—are—not dead?"

"No," he said, somewhat snappishly; "but I soon shall be if I cannot get off these wet clothes."

Then, to his immense dismay, with a hysterical laugh, poor Irene flung herself upon him, all dripping wet with ice water, kissed him over and over again before he could get breath:

"O professor, professor, I thought I saw you die!"

The poor professor felt he would have given the whole world to have had his instrument in position. "It would have been the highest reading on record," he said to himself. "The complexity of conflicting emotions would have put the instrument to a higher test than will ever recur again."

"Brain fever, I fear," said he, as, grasping Irene firmly with both hands, he led her, talking incoherently about her hero, to her berth, where he delivered her over to the stewardess, telling her to summon the doctor, and keep note of her temperature.

Then he turned to his own berth, and, before he took off his dripping garments, he fixed his instrument on his finger and tried to read the register. But it was too fitful, or his arm was too numb with the bruise on his shoulder, for its record to be valuable. So, calling the steward, he undressed, ate a hearty dinner, and was soon in a sound sleep. But, before he dozed off into unconsciousness, a new and unwonted sensation of mingled regret and desire stole over him.

"Steward," he said, "give me my instrument. I want to measure—" but before he finished the sentence, he had dropped off to sleep.

3

THE WHITE GHOST OF DISASTER

MAYN CLEW GARNETT

The main interest in Garnett's story, "The White Ghost of Disaster," is that it was written only a short time before the *Titanic* sank. It ran in the *Popular Magazine,* a U.S. periodical of the pulp variety, in May 1912. The issue, however, was in press before the *Titanic*'s April disaster.

The story is a sad one, with little to recommend it except that as popular fiction goes it is not as bad as most. It tells how the *Admiral,* a gigantic liner sailing the great circle joining New York City and Liverpool, struck a monstrous iceberg in broad daylight, on a calm sea. The ship was 800 feet long, the same size as Robertson's *Titan,* and carried more than a thousand passengers. Most of them perished because of inadequate lifeboats.

When the *Admiral* hit the iceberg it was going 22.5 knots, the exact speed of the *Titanic.* Unlike the *Titanic,* it struck head-on, plowing 100 feet into the ice. Forward bulkheads shattered, and the liner sank in fifteen minutes.

Ian Stevenson was not aware of this story when he wrote his two papers on precognition of the *Titanic* disaster, and I had the pleasure of sending him a copy. In some ways it is a more surprising example of coincidence than Robertson's short novel because of its close proximity in time to the *Titanic* wreck. From my point of view, the story reinforces the fact that many writers, well informed about the dangers of icebergs, were led to tell of big liners meeting their doom in the North Atlantic by ramming "white ghosts."

I have been unable to learn anything about the author. The editors of *Popular Magazine,* introducing the story, mention other tales by him and refer to him as Chief Mate Garnett. I would welcome hearing from anyone who can supply biographical information.

The White Ghost of Disaster

MAYN CLEW GARNETT

Captain Brownson came upon the bridge. It was early morning, and the liner was tearing through a smooth sea in about forty-three north latitude. The sun had not yet risen, but the gray of the coming daylight showed a heaving swell that rolled with the steadiness that told of a long stretch of calm water behind it. The men of the morning watch showed their pale faces white with that peculiar pallor which comes from the loss of the healthful sleep between midnight and morning. It was the second mate's watch, and that officer greeted the commander as he came to the bridge rail where the mate stood staring into the gray ahead.

"See anything?" asked the master curtly.

"No, sir—but I smell it—feel it," said the mate, without turning his head.

"What?" asked Brownson.

"Don't you feel it?—the chill, the—well, it's ice, sir—ice, if I know anything."

"Ice?" snarled the captain. "You're crazy! What's the matter with you?"

"Oh, very well—you asked me—I told you—that's all."

The captain snorted. He disliked the second officer exceedingly. Mr. Smith had been sent him by the company at the request of the manager of the London office. He had always picked his own men, and he resented the office picking them for him. Besides, he had a nephew, a passenger aboard, who was an officer out of a berth.

"What the devil do they know of a man, anyhow! I'm the one responsible for him. I'm the one, then, to choose him. They won't let me shift blame if anything happens, and yet they sent me a man I know nothing of except that he is young and strong. I'll wake him up

127

some if he stays here." So he had commented to Mr. Wylie, the chief mate. Mr. Wylie had listened, thought over the matter, and nodded his head sagely.

"Sure," he vouchsafed; "sure thing." That was as much as any one ever got out of Wylie. He was not a talkative mate. Yet when he knew Smith better, he retailed the master's conversation to him during a spell of generosity engendered by the donation of a few high balls by Macdowell, the chief engineer. Smith thanked him—and went his way as before, trying to do the best he could. He did not shirk duty on that account. Wylie insisted that the captain was right. A master was responsible, and it was always customary for him to pick his men as far as possible. Besides, as Wylie had learned from Macdowell, Brownson had a nephew in view that would have filled the berth about right—so Wylie thought—and Smith was a nuisance. Smith had taken it all in good part, and smiled. He liked Wylie.

Brownson sniffed the air hungrily as he stood there at the bridge rail. The air was chilly, but it was always chilly in that latitude even in summer.

"How does she head?" he asked savagely of the man at the steam-steering gear. The man spoke through the pilot-house window in a monotone:

"West—three degrees south, sir."

"That's west—one south by standard?" snapped Brownson.

"Yes sir," said Smith.

"Let her go west—two south by binnacle—and mark the time accurately," ordered Brownson.

He would shift her a bit. The cool air seemed to come from the northward. It was as if a door in an ice box were suddenly opened and the cold air within let out in a cold, damp mass. A thin haze covered the sea. The side wash rolled away noisily, and disappeared into the mist a few fathoms from the ship's side. It seemed to thicken as the minutes passed.

Brownson was nervous. He went inside the pilot house and spoke to the engineer through the tube leading to the engine room.

"How is she going?"

"Three hundred and ten, sir; never less than three and five the watch."

"Well, she's going too almighty fast—shut her down to two hundred," snapped Brownson. "She's been doing twenty-two knots—it's too fast—too fast, anyhow, in this weather. Ten knots will do until the sun scoffs off this mist. Shut her down."

The slowing engines eased their vibrations, and the side wash rolled less noisily. There was a strange stillness over the sea. The silence grew as the headway subsided.

The captain listened intently. He felt something.

There is always that strange something that a seaman feels in the presence of great danger when awake. It has never been explained. But all good—really good—masters have felt it; can tell you of it if they will. It is uncanny, but it is as true as gospel. The second officer had felt it in the air, felt it in his nerves. He felt—*ice*. It was danger.

Smith stood there watching the haze that seemed to deepen rather than disperse as the morning grew. The men turned out and the hose was started, the decks were sluiced down, and the gang with the squeegees followed. Two bells struck—five o'clock. Smith strained his gaze straight into the haze ahead. He fixed and refixed his glasses—a pair of powerful lenses of fifteen lines. He had bought them for fifty dollars, and always kept them near him while on watch.

A man came up the bridge steps.

"Shall I send up your coffee, sir?" he asked.

"Yes, send it up," said Smith, in a whisper. He was listening.

Something sounded out there in the haze. It was a strange, vibrating sound, a sort of whispering murmur, soft and low, like the far-away notes of a harp. Then it ceased. Smith looked at the captain who stood within the pilot-house window gazing down at the men at work on the deck below. The noise of the rushing water from the hose and their low tones seemed to annoy him. They wore rubber boots, and their footsteps were silent; but he gruffly ordered the bos'n to make them "shut up."

"Better slow her down, sir—there's ice somewhere about here," said the second mate anxiously. He was thinking of the thousand and more souls below and the millions in cargo values.

"Who's running this ship—me or you?" snarled Brownson savagely.

It was an unnecessary remark, wholly uncalled for. Smith flushed under his tan and pallor. He had seldom been spoken to like that. He would have to stand it; but he would hunt a new ship as soon as he came ashore again. It was bad enough to be treated like a boy; but to be talked to that way before the men made it impossible, absolutely impossible. It meant the end of discipline at once. A man would retail it, more would repeat it, and—then—Smith turned away from the bridge rail in utter disgust. He was furious.

"Blast the ship!" he muttered as he turned away and gazed aft. His interest was over, entirely over. He would not have heard a gun fired at that moment, so furious was the passion at the unmerited insolence from his commander.

And then, as if to give insult to injury, Brownson called down the tube:

"Full speed ahead—give her all she'll do—I'm tired of loafing around here all the morning." Then he rang up the telegraph, and the sudden vibrations told of a giant let loose below.

The *Admiral* started ahead slowly. She was a giant liner, a ship of eight hundred feet in length. It took some moments to get headway upon that vast hull. But she started, and in a few minutes the snoring of the bow wave told of a tearing speed. She was doing twenty-two and a half knots an hour, or more than twenty-five miles, the speed of a train of cars.

The under steward came up the bridge steps with the coffee. Smith took his cup and drank it greedily, almost savagely. He was much hurt. His feelings were roughed up to the limit. Yet he had not even answered the captain back. He took his place at the bridge rail and gazed straight ahead into the gray mist. He saw nothing, felt nothing, but the pain of his insult.

"Let him run the ship to hell and back," he said to himself.

There was a puff of colder air than usual. A chill as of death itself came floating over the silent ocean. A man on lookout stood staring straight into the mist ahead, and then sang out.

"Something right ahead, sir," he yelled in a voice that carried like the roar of a gun.

Brownson just seized the lever shutting the compartments, swung it, jammed it hard over, and screamed:

"Stop her—stop her—hard over your wheel—hard over—"

His voice ended in a vibrating screech that sounded wild, weird, uncanny in that awful silence. A hundred men stopped in their stride, or work, paralyzed at the tones coming from the bridge.

And then came the impact.

With a grinding, smashing roar as of thousands of tons coming together, the huge liner plunged headlong into the iceberg that rose grim and silent right ahead, towering over her in spite of her great height. The shock was terrific, and the grinding, thundering crash of falling tons of ice, coupled with the rending of steel plates and solid planks, made chaos of all sound.

The *Admiral* bit in, dug, plowed, kept on going, going, and the whole forward part of her almost disappeared in the wall of white. A thousand tons of huge flakes slammed and slid down her decks, burying her to the fore hatch in the smother. A thousand tons more crashed, slid, and plunged down the slopes of the icy mountain and hurled themselves into the sea with giant splashes, sending torrents of water as high as the bridge rail. The men who had been forward were swept away by the avalanche. Many were never seen again. And then, with reversed engines, she finally came to a dead stop, with her bows jammed a hundred feet deep in the ice wall of the berg.

After that it was panic. All discipline seemed to end in the shock and struggle. Brownson howled and stormed from the bridge, and Smith shouted orders and sprang down to enforce them. The chief mate came on deck in his underclothes and passed the word to man the boats. A thousand passengers jammed the companionway and strove with panic and unhuman fury to reach the deck.

One man clad in a night robe gained the outside of the press, and, running swiftly along the deck, flitted like a ghost over the rail, and disappeared into the sea. He had gone clean crazy, perfectly insane in the panic.

Brownson tied down the siren cord, and the roar shook the atmosphere. The tremendous tones rose above the din of screaming men and cursing seamen; and then the master called down to the heart of the ship, the engine room.

"Is she going?" he asked.

"Water coming in like through a tunnel," came the response. "Nearly up to the grates now—"

That was all. The man left the tube to rush on deck, and the captain knew the forward bulkheads had gone; had either jammed or burst under that terrific impact. The ship was going down.

Brownson stood upon the bridge and gazed down at the human

tide below him. Men fought furiously for places in the small boats. The fireroom crew came on deck and mingled with the passengers. The coal dust showed upon their white faces, making them seem strange beings from an inferno that was soon to be abolished. They strove for places in the lifeboats and hurled the weaker passengers about recklessly. Some, on the other hand, helped the women. One man dragged two women with him into a boat, kicking, twisting, and roaring like a lion. He was a big fellow with a red beard, and Brownson watched him. The mate struck him over the head with a hand spike for refusing to get out of the boat, and his interest in things ended at once and forever.

The crew, on the whole, behaved well. Officers and men tried to keep some sort of discipline. Finally six boats went down alongside into the sea, and were promptly swarmed by the crowds above, who either slid down the falls or jumped overboard and climbed in from the sides. The sea was as still as a lake; only the slight swell heaved it. Great fields of floating particles of ice from the berg floated about, and those who had gotten wet shivered with the cold.

The *Admiral,* running at twenty-two knots an hour, had struck straight into the wall of an iceberg that reached as far as the eye could see in the haze. It towered at least three hundred feet in the air, showing that its depth was colossal, probably at least half a mile. It was a giant ice mountain that had broken adrift from its northern home, and, drifting southward, had survived the heat of summer and the breaking of the sea upon its base.

Smith had felt its dread presence, felt its proximity long before he had come to close quarters. The chill in the air, the peculiar feeling of danger, the icy breath of death—all had told him of a danger that was near. And yet Brownson had scoffed at him, railed at his intuition and sense. Upon the captain the whole blame of the disaster must fall if Smith told.

The second officer almost smiled as he struggled with his boat.

"The pig-headed fool!" he muttered between his set teeth. "The murdering rat—he's done it now! He's killed himself and five hundred people along with him—"

Smith fought savagely for the discipline of his boat. His men had rushed to their stations at the first call. The deck was beginning to slant dangerously as the falls were slacked off and the lifeboat lowered into the sea. Smith stood in the press about him and grew strangely calm. The action was good for him, good for the burning fury that had warped him, scorched him like a hot blast while he had stood silently upon the bridge and taken the insults of his commander. Women pleaded with him for places in the boat. Men begged and took hold of him. One lady, half clothed, dropped upon her knees and, holding his hand which hung at his side, prayed to him as if he were a deity, a being to whom all should defer. He flung her off savagely.

Bareheaded now, coatless, and with his shirt ripped, he stood there, and saw his men pass down sixteen women into his craft; pass them down without comment or favor, age or condition. Thirty souls went into his boat before he sprang into the falls and slid down himself. A dozen men tried to follow him, but he shoved off, and they went into the sea. His men got their oars out and rowed off a short distance.

Muttering, praying, and crying, the passengers in his boat huddled themselves in her bottom. He spoke savagely to them, ordered them under pain of death to sit down. One man, who shivered as he spoke, insisted upon crawling about and shifting his position. Smith struck him over the head, knocking him senseless. Another, a woman, must stand upon the thwarts, to get as far away as possible from the dread and icy element about her. He swung his fist upon her jaw, and she went whimpering down into the boat's bottom, lying there and sobbing softly.

Furiously swearing at the herd of helpless passengers who endangered his boat at every movement, he swung the craft's head about and stood gazing at his ship. After a little while, the crowd became more manageable, and he saw he could keep them aboard without the certainty of upsetting the craft. He had just been debating which of them he would throw overboard to save the rest; save them from their own struggling and fighting for their own selfish ends. He was as cold as steel, hard, inflexible. His men knew him for a ship's officer who would maintain his place under all hazards, and they watched him furtively, and were ready to obey him to the end without question.

"Oh, the monster, the murdering monster!" he muttered again and again.

His eyes were fixed upon the bridge. High up there stood Brownson—the captain who had sent his liner to her death, with hundreds of passengers.

Brownson stood calmly watching the press gain and lose places in the boats. Two boats actually overloaded rolled over under the immense load of human freight. The others did not stop to pick them up. They had enough to do to save themselves. The ship was sinking. That was certain. She must have struck so hard that even the 'midship bulkheads gave way, or were so twisted out of place that the doors failed. The chief engineer came below him and glanced up.

As he did so, a tremendous, roaring blast of steam blew the superstructure upward. The boilers had gone. Macdowell just gave Brownson a look. That was all. Then he rushed for a boat.

Brownson grinned; actually smiled at him.

The man at the wheel asked permission to go.

"I'm a married man, sir—it's no use of me staying here any longer," he ventured.

"Go—go to the devil!" said Brownson, without interest. The man fled.

Brownson stopped giving any more orders. In silence he gazed down at the press of human beings, watching, debating within himself the chances they had of getting away from that scene of death and horror.

The decks grew more and more steep. The liner was settling by the head and to starboard. She was even now twisting, rolling over; and the motion brought down thousands of blocks of ice from the berg. The engines had stopped long since. She still held her head against the ice wall; but it would give her no support. She was slipping away— away to her grave below.

Brownson gazed back over the decks. He watched the crowd impersonally, and it seemed strange to him that so much valuable fabric should go to the bottom so quickly. The paint was so clean and bright, the brass was so shiny. The whole structure was so thoroughly clean, neat, and in proper order. It was absurd. There he was standing upon that bridge where he had stood so often, and here below him were hundreds of dying people—people like rats in a trap.

"Good Heaven—is it real?"

He was sure he was not awake. It must be a dream. Then the terrible knowledge came back upon him like a stroke; a blow that stopped his heart. It was the death of his ship he was watching—the death of his ship and of many of his passengers. Suddenly Brownson saw the boat of the second mate, and that officer standing looking up at him.

The master thought he saw the officer's lips move. He wondered what the man thought, what he would say. He had insulted the officer, made him a clown before the men. He new the second mate would not spare him. He knew the second mate would testify that he had given warning of ice ten minutes before they struck. He also knew that the man at the wheel had heard him, as had the steward who brought up the coffee, and one or two others who were near.

No, there must be no investigation of his, Brownson's, blame in the matter. The master dared not face that. He looked vacantly at Smith. The officer stood gazing straight at him.

The liner suddenly shifted, leaned to starboard, heeled far over, and her bows slipped from the berg, sinking down clear to her decks, clear down until the seas washed to the foot of her superstructure just below Brownson. Masses of ice fell from her into the sea. The grinding, splashing noise awoke the panic again among the remaining passengers and crew. They strove with maniac fury to get the rafts and other stuff that might float over the side. Two boats drew away full to the gunwales with people. The air below began to make that peculiar whistling sound that tells of pressure—pressure upon the vitals of the ship. She was going down.

Brownson still stood gazing at his second mate.

Smith met the master's eye with a steady look. Then he suddenly forgot himself and raised his hand.

"Oh, you murdering rat, you cowardly scoundrel, you devil!" he roared out.

Brownson saw the movement of the hand, saw that it was vindictive, furious, and full of menace. He could not hear the words.

He smiled at the officer, raised his hand, and waved it in reply. It seemed to make the mate crazy. He gesticulated wildly, swore like a maniac—but Brownson did not hear him. He only knew what he was doing.

He turned away, gave one more look over the sinking ship.

"She's going now—and so am I," he muttered.

Then he went slowly into his chart room, opened a drawer, and took out a revolver that he always kept there. He stood at the open door and cocked the weapon. He looked into its muzzle, and saw the bullet that would end his life when he pulled the trigger.

He almost shuddered. It was so unreal. He could not quite do it. He gazed again at the second mate. He knew the officer was watching him, knew Smith would not believe he had the nerve to end the thing then and there. It amused him slightly in a grim sort of way. Why, he *must* die. That was certain. He could never face his own family and friends after what he had done. As to getting another ship—that was too absurd to think of.

The form of a woman showed in the boat. She had risen from the bottom, where the blow of the officer had felled her in her frenzy. Brownson saw her, recognized her as his niece, the sister of the man he had wished to put in Smith's place. It was for his own nephew he had insulted his officer, had caused him to relax and lose the interest that made navigation safe, in the hope that Smith would leave and let his relative get the berth.

He wondered if Smith knew. He stood there with the revolver in his hand watching for some sign from his second officer. Smith gazed at him in fury, apparently not noticing the girl whom he had just before knocked into the boat's bottom to keep order. She stood up. Smith roughly pushed her down again. Brownson was sure now—he felt that Smith knew all.

But he put the revolver in his pocket. He would not fire yet.

The ship was listing heavily, and the cries of the passengers were dying out. All who had been able to get away had gone, somehow, and only a few desperate men and women, who could not swim and who were cool enough to realize that swimming would but prolong an agony that was better over quickly, huddled aft at the taffrail. They would take the last second left them, the last instant of life, and suffer a thousand deaths every second to get it. It was absurd. Brownson pitied them.

Many of these women were praying and talking to their men, who held them in a last embrace. One young woman was clinging closely to a young man, and they were apparently not suffering terror. A look of peacefulness was upon the faces of both. They were lovers, and were satisfied to die together; and the thought of it made them satisfied. Brownson wondered at this. They were young enough and strong enough to make a fight for life.

A whistling roar arose above all other sounds. The siren had ceased, and Brownson knew the air was rushing from below. The ship would drop in a moment. He grasped the pistol again. He dreaded that last plunge, that drop into the void below. The thought held him a little. The ocean was always so blue out there, so clear and apparently bottomless, a great void of water. He wondered at the depth, what kind of a dark bed would receive that giant fabric, the work of so many human hands. And then he wondered at his own end there. His own end? What nonsense! It was unreal. Death was always for others. It had never been for him. He had seen men die. It was not for him yet. He would not believe it. He would awaken soon, and the steward would bring him his coffee.

Then he caught the eye of Smith again in that boat waiting for the end out there. His heart gave an immense jolt, began beating wildly. The ship heeled more and more. The ice crashed and plunged from her forward. Brownson was awakening to the real at last. He felt it in those extra heartbeats; knew he must hurry it. Then he wondered what the papers would say; whether they would call him a coward, afraid to face the inevitable. He hoped they would not. But, then, what difference would it all make, anyhow—to him? He was dead. His interest was over. What difference would it make whether he was a coward or not? Men knew him for what he was, but he was no longer. He was dead.

While he stood there with these thoughts in his mind, his nerve half lacking to end the thing, it seemed to him it was lasting for an eternity. He was growing tired of it all. He turned away again and entered the chart room.

His cat crawled from somewhere and rubbed its tail and side against his leg. Then the animal jumped to the table, and he stroked it; actually stroked it while Smith watched him, and swore at him for a cold-blooded scoundrel.

The ship sank to her superstructure. Her stern raised high in the air. It was now impossible to stand on deck without holding on. Some of the remaining passengers slid off with parting shrieks. They dropped into that icy sea.

Brownson felt the end coming now, and turned again to the doorway, looking straight at his second mate. Smith was trying to quell the movement among his crowd which was endangering his boat again.

The captain clutched the door jamb and watched. Then the ship began to sink. He could not make up his mind to jump clear. There was Smith looking at him. He dared not be saved when hundreds were being killed. No, he could not make that jump and swim to a boat under that officer's gaze. And yet at the last moment he was about to try it. Panic was upon him in a way that he hardly realized. He simply could not face the black gulf he was dropping into with his health and full physical powers still with him. It was nature to make a last effort for his life. Then, before he could make the jump overboard, he saw Smith again shaking his hand at him and howling curses.

He pulled the pistol. An ashy whiteness came over his face. Smith saw it. He stopped swearing; stopped in his furious denunciation of the man who had caused so much destruction. He also saw the pistol plainly, and wondered at the captain's nerve.

"You are afraid, you dog—you are afraid—you daren't do it, you murdering rat!" he yelled.

The men in the boat were all gazing up at the chart-house door where the form of their commander stood.

"He's going to shoot, sir," said the stroke oarsman.

"He's afraid—he won't dare!" howled Smith.

Brownson seemed to hear now. The silence was coming again, and the sounds on the sinking ship were dying out.

Brownson gazed straight at his second officer. Smith saw him raise the pistol, saw a bit of blue smoke, saw his commander sink down to the deck and disappear. A cracking and banging of ice blocks blended with the report, and the ship raised her stern higher. Then she plunged straight downward, straight as a plummet for the bottom of the Atlantic Ocean. Smith knew his captain had gone to his end; that he was a dead man at last.

He stood watching the mighty swirl where the liner had gone under. The men in his boat were also looking. They had seen all.

"Look—look!" shrieked a passenger. "The captain has shot himself!"

"She's gone—gone for good!" cried another. "Oh, the pity of it all!"

Smith did not reply. He was still gazing at the apparition he had seen in that chart-house door; the figure of the man shooting himself through the head. It had chilled his anger, staggered him. The awful nerve of it all, the horror—

"Hadn't we better see if we can get one or two more in her sir?" asked the stroke oarsman. "I see a woman swimming there."

Smith did not answer. He seemed not to hear. Then he suddenly awoke to his surroundings. He was alive to the occasion, the desperate situation.

"Give way port—ease starboard—swing her out of that swirl—hard on that port oar," he ordered.

II.

Smith looked around for the other boats. The chief mate's was in sight, showing dimly through the haze. She was full of people, crowded, and it was a wonder how she floated with the screaming, panic-stricken passengers, who fought for places in her in spite of Wylie's oaths and entreaties. Smith glared.

"The fools!" he muttered. "If they would only think of something besides their own hides for a second. But they won't. They never do. It's nature, and when the trouble comes they fight like cats."

He steered away from what he saw was trouble. He would not pick up the scuffle when they overturned the boat. He was full up now, carrying all his boat would hold. She rocked dangerously with every shifting of the crowd, that still trembled and scuffled for more comfort in her. Her gunwales were only a few inches above the sea, and it might come on to blow at any minute.

"Sit down!" he roared to the old man, who would shift and squirm about in the boat, interfering with the stroke oarsman, who jammed his oar into the small of the fellow's back, regardless of the pain it caused.

"Sit down or I'll throw you overboard! Do you hear?"

The old man whimpered and struggled for a more comfortable position; and Smith reached over with the tiller and slammed him heavily across the shoulders, knocking him over.

"If you get up again I'll kill you, you cowardly old rat!" he said savagely.

The old man lay quiet and trembling. A young woman upbraided Smith for brutality and talked volubly.

"Talk, you little fool!" he said. "Talk all you want to, but don't you get moving about in this boat, or I'll break your pretty neck."

"You are a monster," said the girl.

"Yes; but if I'd had my way, you would have been safe and sound below in your room instead of out here in this ice," snapped Smith.

The girl quieted down, and then spoke to the young woman, who lay in the bottom of the boat where she had fallen when Smith struck her down. She was the niece of Captain Brownson.

"I never heard of such utter brutality in my life," she said.

Miss Billings, who had first found fault, agreed with her.

"Was your brother aboard, Miss Roberts?" asked Smith.

"Yes, he was—I think he went in the mate's boat—why do you ask?"

"Oh, I was just thinking—that's all. He would have been second officer next voyage. That seemed to be fixed, didn't it?"

"Yes; and if it had, this thing would not have happened," said the girl.

"No; probably it would not," said the second officer sadly. He spoke, for the first time, with less passion. He thought of the manner they had taken to get his berth, the insults, the infamy of the whole thing.

"No; I don't suppose you knew how it was done," said he, half aloud.

The girl sat up. She had stopped whimpering from the blow.

Smith watched her for a few minutes while he swung the boat's head for the gray mist ahead where he knew lay the iceberg. He thought the face pretty, the figure well rounded and perfectly shaped. He felt sorry he had used such harshness in making her behave in the boat. But there was no time for silly sentiment. That boat must be manned properly and kept afloat, and the slapping of a girl was nothing at all. She might start a sudden movement and endanger the lives of all. Absolute trimming of the craft was the only way she could be safe to carry the immense load. The men rowed slowly and apparently without object. Smith headed the boat for the ice.

A long wall of peculiar pale blueness suddenly burst from the haze close to them. It was the iceberg. He swung the boat so that she would not strike it and followed along the ragged side.

The two young women gazed up at the pale blueness caused by the fresh water in the ice. It was a beautiful sight. The pinnacles were sharp as needles, and they pierced the mist in white points, tapering down to the white-and-blue sheen at the base, where the ocean roared and surged in a deep-toned murmur. Great pieces broke from the mass while they gazed. Smith steered out and sheered the boat's head away from the dangerous wall. It was grand but deadly. A large block lay right ahead.

"Ease starboard," he said.

The craft swung clear. The mist from the cold ocean thinned a little. Right ahead was a flat plateau, a raised field of ice joining the berg. It sloped down suddenly to the sea, and the swell broke upon it as upon a rocky shore. A long flat floe stretched away from the higher part. It was a field of at least a half mile in length. The huge berg reached a full half mile farther. The whole was evidently broken from some giant glacier in the Arctic.

Smith debated his chances within himself. He scorned to ask his men, for he had seen much ice before in his seagoing. To remain near the berg was to miss a ship possibly; but to row far off was to miss fresh water. He had come away without either food or water, owing to the furious panic. He knew very well that, within a few hours at most, the famished folk in his boat would rave for a drink. They must have water, at least, even if they must do without food.

The iceberg lay right in the path of ships, as his own had proved, the liner running upon the great circle from New York to Liverpool. There was the certainty of meeting, or of at least coming close to a vessel shortly, for others of his line would run the same circle, the same course, as he had run it before.

With giant liners going at twenty-five knots speed, they usually kept pretty close to the same line, for there were few currents that were not accurately known over that route. The Gulf Stream was a fixed unit almost; and in calm weather other ships would certainly reckon with accuracy to meet its set. If he rowed far off the line, then he might or might not meet a ship. If he did not, then there would soon be death and terror in that boat.

He decided to keep close to the berg, and ordered his men to give way slowly while he navigated the field and skirted it, keeping just far enough out to avoid the dangerous breaks and floating pieces.

The morning wore away, and the occupants of his boat began to grow restless. They had been cramped up for several hours now, and they were not used to sitting in a cold, open boat in a thick, misty haze without food or water. The old man began to complain. Several women began to ask for water. One woman with three children begged him to go ashore and get them a piece of ice to allay their thirst. Smith saw that the effects of the wild excitement were now being felt, and the inevitable thirst that must follow was at hand.

He headed the boat for a low part of the field.

"Easy on your oars," he commanded. The boat slid gently upon the sloping ice.

"Jump out, Sam," he said to the bow oarsman. "Jump out and take the painter with you." The man did so, hauling the line far up the floe.

One by one the rest were allowed to climb out of the boat. They gathered upon a part of the field that rose a full ten feet above the sea; and there they began trying to get small pieces of ice to eat. It was as salt as the sea itself, and they were disappointed, spitting it out. Smith took a man along with him and started for the berg. The boat was left in charge of four men, who held her off the floe.

Within half an hour, the whole crowd had managed to get fresh-water ice. The second officer kept them close to the boat and watched for any signs of change in the weather. They were allowed to go a short distance and get the stiffness from their limbs by exercise.

"I am very tired and cold. Can I get back into the boat?" asked Miss Roberts, after she had been stamping her feet upon the floe for half an hour.

Smith looked at her. The print of his hand was plainly marked upon her face. He felt ashamed.

"Yes, you can go aboard," he said; and then, as if in apology for what he had done, he explained: "You must keep quiet in that boat, you know. You must not try to walk about, for it endangers the whole crowd. You understand, don't you?"

"Yes, I'll try and keep still, but my feet get so cold and I grow so stiff."

"Well, you must forgive me for having used you roughly. I had to do it. There was not time for politeness in that panic." He came close to her. His eyes held a light she feared greatly and she shrank back.

"I hope it is not time now for politeness," she said, with meaning.

"Oh, I wouldn't hurt you," said Smith.

"I hope not," said the girl.

Miss Billings asked if she could go aboard also. Smith allowed her, and called the boat in.

The two girls climbed into the boat, and the older women commented spiritedly upon the favors of youth. Smith shut them up with an oath. The woman with the three children huddled them back aboard as the ice caused them to shiver with the cold on their little feet. They had neglected to put on their shoes. The women, for the most part, were only half dressed, and few, if any, had on shoes. They had rushed on deck at the first alarm, and the time allowed for dressing was short. The ship had gone down within fifteen minutes from the first impact with the berg.

Smith walked to and fro upon the ice for some time. The sun shone for a few moments, but was quickly hidden again in the haze.

A gentle breeze began to blow from the southward, and the haze broke up a little. Smith began to get nervous about the ice, and finally ordered all his people back into the boat, where they huddled and shivered, hungry but no longer thirsty.

During all these hours there had been no further sign of the other boats. Smith knew that at least ten of them had gone clear of the sinking ship. The chief mate's boat was the one he was most interested in at present. He wanted to see the man who had indirectly caused the disaster; the man whom Brownson was playing up for the berth of second officer. The thing was a reality now since the tragedy. Before it, he had looked upon the matter as slight indeed.

The second mate headed his boat out and kept clear of the drifting ice but always under the lee of the berg, which offered considerable shelter from both wind and sea, which were rising. The danger of floating ice was not great during daylight, and he swung the small boat close and rode easily, keeping her dry and clear of water. He dreaded the plunging he must inevitably undergo in the open ocean with that load of women.

With the increasing breeze, the haze lifted entirely until the horizon showed clear all around. There was no sign of the other boats. Smith knew then that they had steered off to the southward to avoid the ice. As the sea began to grow, the masses of ice broke adrift with distinct and loud reports, the plunging pieces from the higher parts making considerable noise above the deepening roar of the surge upon the base.

At three in the afternoon, Smith began to feel nervous. The ice was breaking up fast, and immense pieces were floating in the sea which bore them toward him. They grew more and more dangerous to the small craft, and the officer headed away from the vicinity and sought the open at last.

By five that afternoon, when the light was fading, he was riding a heavy sea, that grew rapidly and rolled quickly, the combers breaking badly and keeping two men busy bailing the boat. She made water fast.

The night came on with all its terrors, and the small boat was in great danger. Smith tried his best to keep her headed to the sea, which was now running high and strong. His men began to weaken under the continuous strain; and by ten that night they could no longer hold the boat's head to the sea. She fell off once or twice, and nearly filled when in the trough. There was little to do but make a last effort to hold her. The steady second officer came to his last resource.

There were five oars in the boat. Four of these he lashed into a drag by fastening two of them in the shape of a cross, and then lashing the other two across the end of the cross. He had a spare line of some length in the boat; and with this bent to the painter, he had a cable of at least twenty fathoms, which he led over the bows and to the drag. The drag was weighted with some chain that lay forward. The fifth oar he kept aboard, and used it himself for a sweep to hold her head as nearly as possible behind the drag and to the sea.

He was tired, sore, and hungry, but he kept the boat's head true for hours, and his people huddled down in the bottom, and prayed or swore as the humor took them. The children wept, and some of the older women fainted and lay prone. These gave no trouble. Some of the younger ones still insisted on moving about, and brought the wrath of the mate upon them in no uncertain manner. Smith was making a fight for their lives, and would not tolerate any hysteria. He smote all who disobeyed with his usual impersonal and rough manner; but the two girls were now too much cowed to give him trouble. They lay in the boat's bottom and wept and sobbed the night long, holding to each other, while the boat tossed high in the air or fell far down the slopes of ugly seas, and all the time the water broke over her low gunwales as she sat well down under her load of living freight.

It was about midnight when the old man, who had been unruly

from the first, sprang upon a thwart and plunged over the side with a shrill scream.

Smith saw him, and made a pass to catch him with the oar; but the old fellow drifted out of reach. The second officer swung the boat as far as possible toward him; but still he could not reach the figure that showed floating for a few moments in the darkness. Then Miss Roberts, who was close to the stern sheets, spoke up.

"Oh, the pity of it, the pity of that old man dying like this! Will no one save him?" she cried.

Her companion sat up.

"There's no one aboard here who can do anything but bully us women. If we had a man here, we might save him. I would jump after him myself, but I can't swim. It's horrible to see him drown right alongside of us in this darkness."

Smith heard and smiled grimly. He was tired out, sore, and almost exhausted, but he was full of pluck and fight still. To drop the steering oar might prove fatal if a comber struck the boat. He called to the stroke oarsman who took the oar. Smith took the stern line, gave a turn about a cork jacket that lay upon the seat, and then over the side he went, calling the men to haul him in when he gave the word.

The affair had only taken a few moments, and the form of the old fellow was hardly under the surface. Smith floundered to him; but, being a poor swimmer, as most sailors are, he was quite exhausted when he finaly grabbed him. Instead of easing on the line, he hung dead upon it, hardly able to keep his face out of the sea. The girls watched him over the gunwales, but keeping their places. Two men started to haul him in without waiting for a signal; and they hove upon the line with a right good will. It was old and dry-rotted, as most lines in lifeboats are, and it parted.

Smith felt the slack, and knew what it meant. The cork jacket held him above the surface, and he looked at the boat which seemed so far away in the darkness, but in reality was only a few fathoms. Yet it was too far for him to make it again. It meant his death, his ending.

He tried to swim, but the exertion of the day had been too much. His efforts were weak and ill-directed, and he floundered weakly about, drifting farther away all the time.

The stroke oarsman called for another line. There was none except that of the drag. It would not do to haul it in. The boat was doing all she could now to keep herself afloat, and to risk her broadside in the sea might be fatal for all hands.

Miss Roberts begged some one to go to the officer's assistance. Smith seemed to hear and understand. He floundered with more vigor. There was not a man among the boat's crew who dared to go over the side in the night. There was nothing more to do but watch and hope that the second mate would finally make it. But he did not. He struggled on for many minutes. They could see him now and then fighting silently in the night. He still seemed to hold the old man with one hand.

"It is dreadful—can no one do anything for him?" begged Miss Roberts.

"I can't swim a stroke, lady," said the man at the steering oar.

No one volunteered to go. Smith slowly drifted off as the boat sagged back upon her drag. Then he disappeared entirely in the darkness.

"The brute—I didn't think it was in him," said Miss Billings, with feeling.

"Don't talk that way," said Miss Roberts. "Don't talk that way of a man who did what he has done. I forgive him with all my heart—"

The morning dawned, and the sea rolled with less vigor. The boat was still able to keep herself clear. The white faces of the men told of the frantic endeavor. The women were now nearly all too exhausted to either care for anything or do anything. They lay listless upon the boat's bottom, and she made better weather for that fact. By nine o'clock a steamer was heading for them; and within an hour they were safe aboard and bound in for New York. They arrived a few days later.

The chief mate's boat had kept her course to the southward after leaving the berg—she had gotten ahead of Smith's. By midnight that night she was almost dead ahead of the second officer's boat when Smith jumped in to save the old man.

Daylight showed Wylie a dark speck on the horizon; and at the same time he saw the smoke of the approaching steamer. He had made bad weather of it, also; but with more men and less women in his craft he had kept to the oars, and, when it was very bad, had run slowly before it for several hours. This had brought him from many miles in advance to but a few ahead of Smith's boat; and he was rowing slowly ahead again by daylight. He sighted her, and noticed there were no oars; but he saw the man steering, and rightly guessed that they were hanging onto a drag.

Mr. Roberts, the nephew of Captain Brownson, sat close to the mate. He had relieved him several times during the night. Large and powerful, he was able to aid the chief mate very much.

"I think my sister is in that boat," he said as they sighted her.

"It looks like the second officer's boat, all right," said Wylie.

They rowed straight for her as the smoke of the steamer rose in the east. Before they came within a mile, they saw that the steamer would reach them before they could reach the boat. They then rowed slowly, and watched, waiting.

"Something right ahead, sir," called a man forward.

Roberts looked over the side. He saw something floating.

"Starboard, swing her over a little," he said to the chief mate.

Roberts leaned over the side. He was nervous at what he saw. It had the look of something he dreaded. Then the object came drifting along, and he reached for it. Long before he grasped it, he saw it was the form of a man holding to a cork jacket with one hand and the collar of a man's coat with the other.

The old fellow floated high, and Smith's hand was clenched with a death grip in his clothes. His left hand was jammed through the life jacket, and the fingers clutched the straps. His head lay face upward, and his teeth showed bared from his gums.

"Heavens! It's Smith himself!" exclaimed Roberts. He hauled him aboard with the help of a man.

"It's poor Smith, all right," said Wylie sadly. The life jacket told a tale too plainly. Wylie knew what had happened.

"It's just as well he didn't come ashore. He was guilty, all right," said Mr. Roberts. "A man who wrecks a liner and kills hundreds of passengers might just as well stay out here. Shall we leave him?"

"Not if I know it," said Wylie, with sudden heat.

Within fifteen minutes they were picked up by the steamer and were safe. The manager of the line welcomed Mr. Roberts gladly when that gentleman came to seek him.

"I'm sorry we didn't have you that voyage, Mr. Roberts," he said. "I don't like to say anything against a dead man; but, of course, Smith was on duty when she struck—that is all we know."

"And I suppose you'll want me to go into the other ship, now, sir?" asked the officer.

"Yes, you can report to Captain Wilson any time this week. How is your sister? Did she recover from the boat ride?"

"Well, in a way, but she's forever talking about that blamed second mate, Smith, who seemed to have a strange sort of influence over her while she was with him in the boat. He struck her, too, the dog! It's just as well he didn't come back," said Roberts.

"Well, she'll get over that all right. Smith was a rough sort of man; but as we knew him, he was a first-class sailor, a splendid navigator; and no one seems able to explain how he ran the ship against an iceberg during daylight. It's one of those things we'll never find out. The truth, you know, is mighty hard to fathom in marine disasters. It must have been a terrible blow to Brownson to have to kill himself, unable to face the shame for a mate's offense—but Brownson was always a sensitive man, a splendid fellow; and I suppose he would not go in a boat after what Smith had done. Brownson was captain, and might come under some criticism. Some of the men say he shot himself after upbraiding Smith for his crime."

"Yes. My sister tells me they had quite heated words while the liner was sinking," said the new second mate.

And so William Smith passed out. His name was never mentioned in shipping circles without reserve. But there are still some men who remember him, who knew plain "Bill" Smith, the fighting second officer of the liner that went to her end that morning off the Grand Banks. And those who knew Smith always think of that cork jacket. They made no comment. They knew him. It is not necessary.

4

"A TRYST," AND OTHER POEMS

"A TRYST," AND OTHER POEMS

It is impossible to estimate how many short stories were published around the world before 1912 that described ships going down after hitting icebergs. The same can be said of poems. I would guess that hundreds were published. As far as I know, not one was remotely close to Robertson's novel, or even Garnett's story, in anticipating aspects of the *Titanic* disaster, but these poems reflect how frequently such collisions took place and how much they were feared in the late nineteenth century.

I first came across a reference to Celia Thaxter's poem "A Tryst" in Wyn Craig Wade's book *The Titanic: End of a Dream*. Mrs. Thaxter is a striking example of a poet who was enormously famous in her day but now almost totally unremembered. Some of her books went through more than twenty editions. Her poems were taught in grade schools throughout the country, memorized by students, and reprinted in endless anthologies. I know of no modern anthology that includes a single one of them.

Celia's father, Thomas B. Laighton, was for ten years the keeper of the White Island lighthouse in the Isles of Shoals, off the coast of Portsmouth, New Hampshire. It was there that Celia spent her childhood, and most of her lyrical verse deals with aspects of the sea. Her husband, Levi Lincoln Thaxter, was an expert on the poetry of Robert Browning, and her son Roland Thaxter became a noted professor of botany at Harvard. Celia moved in the highest literary circles, a friend of Thoreau, Whittier, Lowell, and many other famous New England writers.

In 1896, two years after Mrs. Thaxter died on one of the Isles of Shoals, a complete collection of her poems was edited by the Maine writer and poet Sarah Orne Jewett. It is from this edition that I reprint "A Tryst," although the poem was first published some twenty years earlier.

151

As a whimsical example of how easy it is to find coincidences, note that "The Titanic" can be spelled by taking the ten letters in order from among the first nine words of Mrs. Thaxter's poem ("From out the desolation of the North/An iceberg . . ."). I'll wager that readers will have a hard time finding another poem in which this can be done.

A Tryst

Celia Thaxter

From out the desolation of the North
    An iceberg took its way,
From its detaining comrades breaking forth,
    And traveling night and day.

At whose command? Who bade it sail the deep
    With that resistless force?
Who made the dread appointment it must keep?
    Who traced its awful course?

To the warm airs that stir in the sweet South,
    A good ship spread her sails;
Stately she passed beyond the harbor's mouth,
    Chased by the favoring gales;

And on her ample decks a happy crowd
    Bade the fair land good-by;
Clear shone the day, with not a single cloud
    In all the peaceful sky.

Brave men, sweet women, little children bright,
    For all these she made room,
And with her freight of beauty and delight
    She went to meet her doom.

Storms buffeted the iceberg, spray was swept
    Across its loftiest height;
Guided alike by storm and calm, it kept
    Its fatal path aright.

Then warmer waves gnawed at its crumbling base,
    As if in piteous plea;
The ardent sun sent slow tears down its face,
    Soft flowing to the sea.

Dawn kissed it with her tender rose tints, Eve
    Bathed it in violet,
The wistful color o'er it seemed to grieve
    With a divine regret.

Whether Day clad its clefts in rainbows dim
    And shadowy as a dream,
Or Night through lonely spaces saw it swim
    White in the moonlight's gleam,

Ever Death rode upon its solemn heights,
    Ever his watch he kept;
Cold at its heart through changing days and nights
    Its changeless purpose slept.

And where afar a smiling coast it passed,
    Straightway the air grew chill;
Dwellers thereon perceived a bitter blast,
    A vague report of ill.

Like some imperial creature, moving slow,
    Meanwhile, with matchless grace,
The stately ship, unconscious of her foe,
    Drew near the trysting place.

For still the prosperous breezes followed her,
    And half the voyage was o'er;
In many a breast glad thoughts began to stir
    Of lands that lay before.

And human hearts with longing love were dumb,
    That soon should cease to beat,
Thrilled with the hope of meetings soon to come,
    And lost in memories sweet.

Was not the weltering waste of water wide
    Enough for both to sail?
What drew the two together o'er the tide,
    Fair ship and iceberg pale?

There came a night with neither moon nor star,
    Clouds draped the sky in black;
With fluttering canvas reefed at every spar,
    And weird fire in her track,

The ship swept on; a wild wind gathering fast
    Drove her at utmost speed.
Bravely she bent before the fitful blast
    That shook her like a reed.

O helmsman, turn thy wheel! Will no surmise
    Cleave through the midnight drear?
No warning of the horrible surprise
    Reach thine unconscious ear?

She rushed upon her ruin. Not a flash
    Broke up the waiting dark;
Dully through wind and sea one awful crash
    Sounded, with none to mark.

Scarcely her crew had time to clutch despair,
    So swift the work was done:
Ere their pale lips could frame a speechless prayer,
    They perished, every one!

Here is how Herman Melville dealt with the same theme:

The Berg

A Dream

I saw a ship of martial build
(Her standards set, her brave apparel on)
Directed as by madness mere
Against a stolid iceberg steer,
Nor budge it, though the infatuate ship went down.

The impact made huge ice-cubes fall
Sullen, in tons that crashed the deck;
But that one avalanche was all—
No other movement save the foundering wreck.

Along the spurs of ridges pale,
Not any slenderest shaft and frail,
A prism over glass-green gorges lone,
Toppled; or lace of traceries fine,
Nor pendant drops in grot or mine
Were jarred, when the stunned ship went down.
Nor sole the gulls in cloud that wheeled
Circling one snow-flanked peak afar,
But nearer fowl the floes that skimmed
And crystal beaches, felt no jar.

No thrill transmitted stirred the lock
Or jack-straw needle-ice at base;
Towers undermined by waves—the block
Atilt impending—kept their place.
Seals, dozing sleek on sliddery ledges
Slipped never, when by loftier edges
Through very inertia overthrown,
The impetuous ship in bafflement went down.

Hard Berg (methought), so cold, so vast,
With mortal damps self-overcast;
Exhaling still thy dankish breath—
Adrift dissolving, bound for death;
Though lumpish thou, a lumbering one—
A lumbering lubbard loitering slow,
Impingers rue thee and go down,
Sounding thy precipice below,
Nor stir the slimy slug that sprawls
Along thy dead indifference of walls.

Thomas Hardy, after the loss of the *Titanic*, penned these stanzas:

The Convergence of the Twain

In a solitude of the sea
Deep from human vanity,
And the Pride of Life that planned her, stilly couches she.

Steel chambers, late the pyres
Of her salamandrine fires,
Cold currents thrid, and turn to rhythmic tidal lyres.

Over the mirrors meant
To glass the opulent
The sea-worm crawls—grotesque, slimed, dumb, indifferent.

Jewels in joy designed
To ravish the sensuous mind
Lie lightless, all their sparkles bleared and black and blind.

Dim moon-eyed fishes near
Gaze at the gilded gear
And query: "What does this vaingloriousness down here?"

Well: while was fashioning
This creature of cleaving wing,
The Immanent Will that stirs and urges everything

Prepared a sinister mate
For her—so gaily great—
A Shape of Ice, for the time far and dissociate.

And as the smart ship grew
In stature, grace, and hue,
In shadowy silent distance grew the Iceberg too.

Alien they seemed to be:
No mortal eye could see
The intimate welding of their later history,

Or sign that they were bent
By paths coincident
On being anon twin halves of one august event.

Till the Spinner of the Years
Said "Now!" And each one hears,
And consummation comes, and jars two hemispheres.

And now, for a less sombre way of closing this curious anthology,
an excerpt from Carl Sandburg's *The People, Yes:*

"Isn't that an iceberg on the horizon, Captain?"
"Yes, Madam."
"What if we get in a collision with it?"
"The iceberg, Madam, will move right along as though nothing
had happened."